# THE THINGS I REMEMBER

*To Judy*

*May God continue to bless you & yours. I pray that you enjoy the book. Thank you former member of the ROBERTS GOSPEL Singers. Lol*

*Be blessed*

*Peterman*

# PETERMAN

## The Things I Remember

### LIVING IN THE VILLAGE
# BELLS MILL
#### BY REV. EDWARD J. WILSON

XULON PRESS

Xulon Press
2301 Lucien Way #415
Maitland, FL 32751
407.339.4217
www.xulonpress.com

© 2022 by Rev. Edward J. Wilson

Edited by Dr. Sarah Williams
Compiled by Kevin Owens

All rights reserved solely by the author. The author guarantees all contents are original and do not infringe upon the legal rights of any other person or work. No part of this book may be reproduced in any form without the permission of the author.

Due to the changing nature of the Internet, if there are any web addresses, links, or URLs included in this manuscript, these may have been altered and may no longer be accessible. The views and opinions shared in this book belong solely to the author and do not necessarily reflect those of the publisher. The publisher therefore disclaims responsibility for the views or opinions expressed within the work.

Unless otherwise indicated, Scripture quotations taken from the King James Version (KJV)–*public domain*.

Unless otherwise indicated, Scripture quotations taken from the Holy Bible, New International Version (NIV). Copyright © 1973, 1978, 1984, 2011 by Biblica, Inc.™. Used by permission. All rights reserved.

Paperback ISBN-13: 978-1-6628-4635-9
Ebook ISBN-13: 978-1-6628-4636-6

# The Things I Remember
## LIVING IN THE VILLAGE
## BELLS MILL

AN AUTOBIOGRAPHY

# TABLE OF CONTENTS

FOREWORD . . . . . . . . . . . . . . . . . . . . . . . . . . . . . . . . . . . . . . . . . . . . .ix
DEDICATION . . . . . . . . . . . . . . . . . . . . . . . . . . . . . . . . . . . . . . . . . . .xi
SPECIAL THANKS . . . . . . . . . . . . . . . . . . . . . . . . . . . . . . . . . . . . xiii
FROM THE AUTHOR THE THINGS I REMEMBER . . . . . . . . . . xv
PREFACE . . . . . . . . . . . . . . . . . . . . . . . . . . . . . . . . . . . . . . . . . . . . .xvii
1. THE BAT CAVE . . . . . . . . . . . . . . . . . . . . . . . . . . . . . . . . . . . . . . 1
2. LIVING IN THE BAT CAVE . . . . . . . . . . . . . . . . . . . . . . . . . . . . 7
3. GREEDY BUTT . . . . . . . . . . . . . . . . . . . . . . . . . . . . . . . . . . . . . 13
4. GETTING MY "EDUMACATION" . . . . . . . . . . . . . . . . . . . . . 17
5. A SILLY QUESTION . . . . . . . . . . . . . . . . . . . . . . . . . . . . . . . . 25
6. THE MIND IS A TERRIBLE THING TO WASTE . . . . . . . . . . 29
7. COME TO JESUS . . . . . . . . . . . . . . . . . . . . . . . . . . . . . . . . . . . 33
8. ANSWERING THE CALL . . . . . . . . . . . . . . . . . . . . . . . . . . . . 39
9. HUMOR IN THE FAMILY . . . . . . . . . . . . . . . . . . . . . . . . . . . 49
10. MRS. SWEETIE . . . . . . . . . . . . . . . . . . . . . . . . . . . . . . . . . . . . 55
11. THE TIE THAT BINDS . . . . . . . . . . . . . . . . . . . . . . . . . . . . . . 59
12. BELLS MILL THE VILLAGE . . . . . . . . . . . . . . . . . . . . . . . . . 71
13. WE'RE MOVING ON UP . . . . . . . . . . . . . . . . . . . . . . . . . . . . 87
14. OVER MY HEAD, I HEAR MUSIC . . . . . . . . . . . . . . . . . . . . 91
15. BLACK & WHITE TOGETHER . . . . . . . . . . . . . . . . . . . . . . 105
16. MY FUTURE WAS DOWNSTAIRS IN THE PING
    PONG ROOM . . . . . . . . . . . . . . . . . . . . . . . . . . . . . . . . . . . . 115
17. WELCOME TO THE REAL WORLD OF
    WORKING . . . . . . . . . . . . . . . . . . . . . . . . . . . . . . . . . . . . . . . 121
18. THE TIRE MAN AT CHESAPEAKE PUBLIC
    SCHOOLS . . . . . . . . . . . . . . . . . . . . . . . . . . . . . . . . . . . . . . . .127
19. I FOUND MY THRILL IN SUNRISE HILL . . . . . . . . . . . . . . 137
20. 2010 THE YEAR OF CHANGE . . . . . . . . . . . . . . . . . . . . . . . 147
EPILOGUE . . . . . . . . . . . . . . . . . . . . . . . . . . . . . . . . . . . . . . . . . . . 157
THE VILLAGE ROLL CALL "AS I KNEW THEM" . . . . . . . . . . . 163

# FOREWORD

# TERESA HILL WILSON

*"Hold fast to dreams, for if dreams die,*
*life is a broken winged bird that cannot fly"*
*by Langston Hughes*

I've known my husband, Rev. Edward J. Wilson, for forty-five years and I'm happy that he is allowing God to use him with his many gifts. As he shares his life experiences being raised in Bells Mill, I hope you will be encouraged in knowing that God blesses us with blessings, both seen and unseen. I found myself laughing at some experiences of his life in this book and at the same time, I could see God developing him to be who he is in Christ and in the capacity of being an anointed minister of music and preacher of the gospel.

He has accompanied many, many choirs and groups over the years. It was through his gift of music that I met him as we have shared our lives together as husband and wife for forty-three years. He has been a mentor to many young musicians locally in gospel music. Through his book, I understand the difference in a community and a village. I can see he had many mothers and fathers who nurtured him and loved him in the village of Bells Mill. My prayer is that the readers of this book will be blessed as my husband shares his life. I love him dearly and I pray that God will continue to use him to be a blessing to others as he has been to our family. Enjoy!

- Min. Teresa Hill Wilson

# DEDICATION

This book is dedicated to my lovely and beautifully spirit-filled wife of forty-three years, Teresa, and to our four beautiful, sweet daughters: Keisha, Sherita, Ashley, and Nikki and our five wonderful grandchildren: Ryan, Aayla, Alayna, Trey, and Rayah. I also have to include my two sons, Monzie and Ray, who are the spouses of my two eldest daughters. These are the inner circle of people in my life whom I love so dearly. We are family and as the Word of God says, "As for me and my house, we will serve the Lord." My desire is that they will know the life of the man they call Baby, Dad, Daddy, Pop, Peter, Grand Daddy, and G.D. I love you guys.

I would also like to give thanks to those who were mothers and fathers to me in the village of Bells Mill. The old saying goes, "It takes a village to raise a child," and in Bells Mill there were so many who played the role of parents to me and so many others raised in Bells Mill. They chastised me, whipped me, and then they sent me home for the laying on of hands by "My" Chief in the Village known as "Sweetie," my mom. Thanks so much to those who may still be here and to those who have transitioned from life on earth to life in heaven.

- Rev. Edward J. Wilson
*aka-Peterman*

# SPECIAL THANKS
*and appreciation to the following:*

MY LORD AND SAVOR JESUS CHRIST
DR. SARAH E. WILLIAMS
MR. STUART ANDERSON
MR. KEVIN OWENS
DR. E. CURTIS ALEXANDER
MR. WILLIAM HOLMES

# FROM THE AUTHOR
# THE THINGS I REMEMBER

My name is Edward James Wilson, and I was born on September 16, 1955, in DePaul Hospital located in Norfolk, Virginia. Two months and twenty days before Mrs. Rosa Parks refused to give up her seat to a white man, I was born to Mrs. Sweetie Alberta Wilson and Mr. Edward Marvin Ashby at 8:49 a.m. on a rain filled Friday morning.

I really don't feel that my biography is "ALL THAT," but I would like to share with you the things I remember about my life, which made me the person I am. My strengths, weaknesses, my ups, my downs, my smiles, and my frowns, these memories may not be important or significant to you, but they are precious to me and the thoughts I have of my past put a smile on my face and in my heart. I lived a good and disciplined life in a loving village.

Living in a world so different from our world today because of our ever-changing society, I find myself looking back and recognizing how good God was and still is to me. My past is the evidence of the reality of God and His favor in my life. From adventure to adventure, from year to year, from page to page, I found that this Spiritual Being, this Holy Personality whom we call God was, is, and forever will be the giver and sustainer of my life. God has been "THE" light in my darkest days. My mother, grandmother, and

# THE THINGS I REMEMBER

aunts all taught me to trust in the Lord, love the Lord, and accept the Lord as my personal savior. Some things I talk about may be remembered differently by others, but I must tell things according to "my" remembrance. I have no complaints about my childhood. I lived an exciting life involving many great people who lived in the Village of Bells Mill. I will never forget where I've come from and will forever praise God for where I am today with my beautiful wife and our four beautiful daughters along with our five wonderful grandchildren. It is my past that molded me to become "Peterman from Bells Mill." I am not much but such as I am to God be the glory. Nikki Giovanni once said the following of white people writing about her,

*"White folks may talk about how poor we were and talk about my horrible childhood. We had our loved ones and we had happy birthdays and very Merry Christmases. These folks don't understand that black love is black wealth, and they will talk about my horrible childhood and never understand that all the while I was quite happy."*

God's grace is sufficient to keep me. I "AM" worthy of His blessings because I am His and He is mine and it is only by his grace that I am here. I may go back and forward in time, but this is my story. Thank you, family, and neighbors, from the Village of Bells Mill for being a mother to me when my mom was working and a father to me when I needed one. Thank you, God, for allowing me to be raised in "THE VILLAGE" called Bells Mill. I thank you, God for molding just for me, my angel, Teresa L. Hill, and for allowing us to be the parents of four beautiful daughters who have blessed us with five beautiful loving grandchildren so far. God has been and is so good to me.

- Rev. Edward J. Wilson
*aka-Peterman*

# PREFACE

Bells Mill is, or should I say was, a small Black community located in the southern part of what was Norfolk County, but today it is called Chesapeake, Virginia. I said it "was" a small black community because the demographics have changed over the past few years and a more diverse population now resides in the small community, with a handful of black residents. In addition, white families have purchased many of the homes once occupied by Black families. Some homes have been demolished or renovated. Through research, I found that Bells Mill was established around the 1870s by such men as Mr. Henry Bell, a descendent of the Bells who were residents of Bells Mill during my childhood, and some are still in Bells Mill today.

There was a sawmill at the end of what is now called Progress Drive in Bells Mill called Sawyers Mill. The name was later changed to Richmond Cedar Works. This sawmill employed many men who lived in and around the area and some who lived in North Carolina. On the corner of Progress Drive and Bells Mill Road stood a large two-story building, a boarding house, for those who worked at the sawmill during the week and went home on the weekends. Research revealed that some families, such as the Bells, the Corprews, the Jones, and the Alexanders, and others purchased a great deal of land, and that land was given and sold to other

## THE THINGS I REMEMBER

relatives and families in Bells Mill. Some of the property extended from Bells Mill Road to Cedar Road, covering acres and acres.

An Afro Union Civil War Soldier named Sgt. March Corprew, was a descendent of the Alexanders, who purchased 200 acres of land that stretched from the Alexander/McDonald Cemetery to what is now called Alexander Lane. It went back from Bells Mill Road to what is now called Cedar Road. Sgt. Corprew donated twenty acres of land to Norfolk County in 1922 to build a School for colored children. This original school was built in 1923, and it was later to become Bells Mill Elementary School, which I attended.

Bells Mill was more of a village than a community during my upbringing simply because it was a place where everyone was your parents, and most adults had the" right" to discipline any child and send them home for more discipline from their parents. Our neighbors loved us as though we were their own children. Professional men and women in Bells Mill served their places of employment and implemented their gifts and talents to help those in the community and the various churches. Mr. Charles Davis had his own plumbing business. Mr. William Bell was a certified contractor who built homes; Mr. Colon Simmons and Mr. Cecil Bell, and Mr. Sam Coker were professional barbers and owned their barbershop. Then you had teachers and professors, nurses such as my Aunt Laura Eason. Later, you will hear about the post offices and the fish market and the convenience stores and churches in Bells Mill. I remember hearing Mr. Roosevelt Chesson whistling the song "Blessed Assurance" as he walked down the street with his working cart. He was a well-respected neighborhood handyman through the week, but to see him on Sundays, as most of the men in our village, one would think he was the mayor of Bells Mill.

To locate Bells Mill, I would say that it was the bologna between two slices of bread. The top slice is Great Bridge, and the second slice is Grassfield/Deep Creek. In between is the meat of the sandwich, Bells Mill. When I drive through Bells Mill today and see the change that has occurred both in the current homes and the occupants, I realize that God speaks a message. If we can't live together down here, then how can we live together up in heaven? Therefore, He allowed Bells Mill to be transformed from a village to a community. We are all God's children, red and yellow, black, and white, we are all precious in His sight. I praise God for honoring me by allowing me the privilege of saying that I am a product of the village called Bells Mill. Bells Mill was and will forever be my home.

# 1.

# THE BAT CAVE

I remember the two-story house located at 729 Luther Street in the Bells Mill section of Chesapeake, Virginia, formally known as Norfolk County. My uncle, Ovid Nichols, who passed away in his eighties on March 18, 2009, was born in this house. My cousin and pastor, Sarah Eason Williams, was also born in this same house over sixty years ago. As I recall, this house was once cream-colored with ceramic tile on each side of the house. Later, it was painted pink. I remember the screened-in front porch with the old velvet-like sofa on it. I also recall a swing on the front porch attached by hooks on the porch's ceiling. I remember those hot summer nights sitting on the screened-in front porch, hearing the crickets and the sight of the lightning bugs as they flew around outside. When you walk in the front door from the front porch, there was a hallway. Then, straight ahead to the right, a staircase took you upstairs to two large bedrooms and a smaller room, which was once occupied by my grandmother and later used for storage.

To the left of the staircase downstairs was a hallway that led to two doors on the left side. The first door you entered was the "living" room, "where nobody lived." This room was often cold since we only used the space during Christmas. Keeping the door closed prevented cold air from escaping from the room to other parts of the house. In this room, there was a sofa, a big living room chair, a wood/coal heater, and an old upright piano donated to me by my mom's church, Lee's Chapel AME Church.

The next hallway door on the left led you into my aunt and uncle's bedroom. Another doorway also connected this room to the aforementioned living room, which was used only at Christmas. This doorway was blocked off using a bed sheet to preserve the heat in the bedroom. After my uncle and aunt bought their own home in the early sixties, my mom and I moved downstairs into this bedroom. I remember my mom's room always being clean with fresh linen on the bed, smelling like the fresh air outdoors because all the linen had been washed and hung outside on the clothesline. I remember the mirrored dresser and the chest drawer in the bedroom. I also remember the "slop jar" or the "pail," a white metal bucket with a handle that we used as a bathroom commode. We used this metal bucket because we had no indoor plumbing. My job was to take the "used" pail to the outdoor toilet about thirty yards behind the main house. The outdoor bathroom was a little house made of wood measuring about six feet by six feet with a floor covering a hole in the ground. Over the hole was a wooden commode for waste to go down. One of my chores was to clean the pail with bleach, bring it back into the house, and put it back at the foot of the bed. I remember those summer nights going to the outdoor toilet to use the bathroom. I'd take my little transistor radio, a flashlight, and the newspaper to the bathroom and take my time in the dark reading what was to become my toilet paper. Then, all of a sudden, I'd imagine a snake crawling up the toilet seat and pecking my butt, so off I went, sometimes cutting things short.

Another chore I had was chopping wood. I would go outside after coming home from school, change my clothes, grab the ax, go outside to the woodpile, and chop wood. I would try to be slick, piling the wood up like the Indian's tope, giving a false impression that I had cut a big pile of wood. Mama Creasy (my grandmother) would come outside, take the ax and knock the stack down flat and say, "Boy, you ain't chopped enough wood, I'm gonna tell your mammy when she git' home." She would tell my mom, and of course, I received my whipping for trying to be slick with the wood. As I was getting a whipping, my grandmother would get mad at my mom for whipping me. This event would repeat itself later in my adult life when my mom moved into my home with my family and me. My mom would give me a report about my children's behavior, and when I spanked them, my mom would get upset with me.

After my aunt and uncle moved to their new house, my grandmother moved downstairs in the dining room/den. My grandmother, Mrs. Creasy Williams, slept on a sleep sofa in this room. Other furnishings in this room included an oversized black reclining rocking chair, a small television mounted on a tall table, a wood-coal heater, and a dining table that served as a getaway spot for me and my cousins Sarah and Rona (Verona) during thunderstorms. During thunderstorms, we took shelter under this antique table.

The last room downstairs was the kitchen. Our kitchen consisted of a wood cookstove with an overhead food warmer attached, a kitchen table, a refrigerator, and a kitchen sink. Even though we had no indoor plumbing, we used an old hand pump to get water. Once you primed the pump and the water came, it would go into the kitchen sink, which had a pipe that ran the water outside into a ditch near the outdoor toilet. On the "back" porch was a pile of wood that I had chopped for heating and cooking. Behind our house was a pile of coal for heating. With no "running water" in the "BAT CAVE," bathing required pumping water into a foot tub and placing the foot tub on the wood stove in the kitchen to warm up the water. Although we had no indoor bathroom, we kept ourselves clean. Yes, we stayed clean with no showers or bathtubs.

I learned from my cousins that in the beginning, my mom and I had the front bedroom upstairs. In the back bedroom were my cousins Eddie, Jackie, Rona, and Sarah. I'm told that my cousin

# THE THINGS I REMEMBER

Jackie was given the task every morning by mother, who was on her way to work, to get out of her warm bed and get into the bed with me. Jackie has reminded me over the years of her climbing in bed with her "big headed" baby cousin. I also confirmed that the small storage room was where our grandmother, Mama Creasy, slept. Before moving to their new home, Uncle Arthur and Aunt Laura Eason slept in the bedroom downstairs, where my mom and I later occupied. After the Eason's built their own house at 932A Aberdeen Lane, Sweetie and I moved into the bedroom downstairs previously occupied by Uncle Arthur and Aunt Laura. As stated before, Mama Creasy moved down into the dining room/den on a sleeping couch, and my Uncle Lloyd moved in with us, and he began to sleep upstairs.

My mother was a domestic worker for years, working in the homes of "White folks," ironing, washing, and cleaning. Most of the clothes I had were hand-me-downs from her employers' children. Even a lot of the toys I got came from her White employers. I remember one of my favorites, a little red and white record player with little kiddy records. Man, the fun I had with that record player. I remember getting a swing set with a sliding board, also from her employer. I thought I was at an amusement park with that sliding board and those three rusty swings.

I remember so many things living in the "BAT CAVE" at 729 Luther Street, but two things stand out most in my heart: the love that my cousins and I received and the fact that we were poor but didn't know it. We always had food, shelter, were taught the things of God and were seriously disciplined. For example, if you didn't go to church, you didn't go outside to play on Sundays. What a wonderful life I lived in the "BAT CAVE.

Why do I call our home the "BAT CAVE?" We had bats flying in and out of the attic of our home as the sun went down. They took up residence in our attic and would sometimes manage to get into the rooms in the house. I can remember my mom and

Uncle Lloyd, my mom's brother, grabbing a broom and slamming the door as they chased and killed bats, knocking them out of the air. I even recall my uncle Lloyd once killing a bat with his bare hands. I remember my mom chasing a flying bat with a broom swinging the broom-like Jackie Robinson swinging a baseball bat. She always managed to hit a home run with the poor bat lying on the floor saying, "Who 'IS' that woman?" My mom once knocked a home run with a bat, and he landed on her pretty snow-white blanket on the bed. She told me that the bat looked so cute and velvet-like on the bright white sheet. She said, "Edvard (that's how she pronounced Edward, the name "SHE" gave me) you've got the mark of a bat on your hands. That's why your hands look so silky and velvet-like" As we say in the Black church, "The devil IS a lie. I ain't got the mark of no bat in my hands." (Oh, excuse me, I got caught up there). Our house at 729 was the home of the Easons, the Wilsons, the Williams, and the bats. Folk would pass our house ducking these little flying rodents. Everybody knew that 729 Luther Street. in the village of Bells Mill was, in reality, "THE BAT CAVE."

# 2.
# LIVING IN THE BAT CAVE

Precious memories, how they linger! How they ever flood my soul! Not just good memories, not just bad memories, but precious memories. When I think of my first years at 729 Luther Street, I think of the nighttime soap opera "Dallas." The cast of characters included JR, Bobby, Sue Ellen, Pam, Gary, and the whole Ewing clan living in one house. Living at 729, was my grandmother, my mother, my aunt, and uncle and their four children, and somewhere in the house was Uncle Lloyd. Around 1962, the Easons like Gary Ewing moved into their new home located within walking distance at 932A Aberdeen Lane.

I can't remember our daily food for dinner during the weeknights, but I remember that Sunday's dinner was prepared on Saturday night. Therefore, Sunday's breakfast consisted of eggs, grits, and a piece of fried chicken deducted from Sunday's dinner. I remember my cousin Sarah (now my pastor) having nose bleeds on Sunday mornings during breakfast. As much as I loved her like a sister, it never ruined my appetite. Sunday's dinner consisted of soul food, of course; fried chicken, cabbage, macaroni and cheese, potato salad, stringed beans, and red Kool-Aid in our Flintstone drinking glasses. Man, I can taste that Kool-Aid now. The chickens were fresh from the chicken house.

# THE THINGS I REMEMBER

I can see Mama Creasy in the backyard with a live chicken in one hand and an ax in the other. I saw her when she laid the chicken's head on a chopping block and swung down the ax on the neck of the chicken. I saw the chicken's head in one direction with its eyes blinking and its mouth moving. In the other direction, its body flapping its feathered wings flying all over the place along with me running in another direction. There was blood flying all over the place and even on my grandmother's apron and dress. What an ugly sight to see, yet a delicious bird to eat. That same chicken was soon cleaned with feathers plucked and fried and took residence in my stomach. That chicken died that I might live. I remember my cousins Verona and Sarah and myself eating Sunday breakfast and dinner. As the adults ate at the big table, we, the children, ate at our small ABC folding table with our little chairs while drinking from those Flintstone glasses. Back in that time, before television remotes, my grandmother and mother had three remotes to our little black & white television with no knobs. When they wanted the channel changed, they would use their three-way remote call, "Rona (Verona), Sarah or Edvard."

After my aunt Laura and her family moved into their new home, I no longer had Sarah and Rona to play with. Rona did stay for a while because of her bond with my mom, whom she called "Aunt Heeay." However, when she moved with her parents, it was just me, my mom, my grandmother, and Uncle Lloyd. It became a lonely life with no kids in the house except me. I was the only kid living in the "BAT CAVE."

Then, on Friday nights, my cousins Sarah Eason and Beverly Williams would spend the weekend with me. Beverly is the daughter of my mom's youngest deceased brother Willis A. Williams Sr. better known as "Peco." I remember how the three of us would squeeze in that big black reclining rocking chair that belonged to my grandmother and watch cartoons like the Flintstones, the Jetsons, the classic Three Stooges, and the Mickey Mouse club.

Then, late Friday nights, we would fearfully look at the scary television show called "SHOCK." This movie program opened with a squeaking sound of a casket door opening, and a man would rise from the coffin and say, "WELCOME TO THE WORLD OF SSHOCCKK!" The show would feature such movies as the old Frankenstein and Wolf Man movies and Dracula and other scary movies in black and white. Friday night dinner was always cheeseburgers, hot dogs, French fries, fish sticks, and apple sauce. Good 'eats' and good times!

The family sometimes referred to the living room I mentioned earlier as the "front room." As stated earlier, the family only used this room during the Christmas holidays, at which time we would light the coal-wood heater. I remember well the old-time Christmas nights. My mom would always put up a Christmas tree, but I never understood why all my buddies had these tall, full Christmas trees, real or artificial, and I always had a half of a tree. While living at 729 Luther Street., our tree sat upon a table covered with a clean white sheet. My cousin, Jackie Eason Wilson, told in later years that her father, my Uncle Arthur, would go into the woods and chop down a cedar tree for us. I loved decorating the Christmas tree with lights, ornaments, icicles, and a can of white snow sprayed on the tree to give it a wintry look. I remember being in that cold room with a blanket over me, gazing longingly at the pretty Christmas tree lights. That image has never left me.

During Christmas time, the houses were lit up with lights on the corner of Bells Mill Rd. and Luther Street. Uncle Peco, his wife, and their seven children had the prettiest, tallest, whitest artificial Christmas tree in their living room window. A blue floodlight was shining on it from the outside. Across from my Uncle Peco's house lived my cousin Lottie and her husband Buster Bell and their children, my cousins Sharon and Juanita. Their house was all lit up with colorful lights around the front of the front porch. Next door was the home of Mr. Cle and his wife, Mrs. Mary Bell, better known as "Ms. Bug." Mr. Cle lit up the house with beautiful Christmas lights around the entire house. On this same corner, across from my Uncle Peco's house, lived Mr. William "Bill" Chesson, his wife, my cousin, Minnie "Doll" Chesson, and their nine children. Their home also had Christmas lights all around the house and a pretty Christmas tree in their big "picture" window.

Further down the street was the home of my friends and buddies Lamont and Larry Simmons and their little sister Pamela who were the kids of Mr. Colon and Mrs. Hilda Simmons. They had this big picture window displaying a tall and wide Christmas tree with heavy icicles hanging from it. You will hear more about these folks later in this book. I am fascinated by Christmas lights and the height of Christmas trees. So, I made a promise that when or if I ever had kids, they would "always" have a big tree. That promise I have kept to this day to my children and my grandchildren.

My mom would put coals and wood in the heater and heat the front room on Christmas mornings, making it warm and cozy. I remember the blue Tonka dump truck, the roller skates that I never learned the art of using, a bicycle with headlights, a bell, blinking lights on the back seat, and my favorite, an eight-shape race car set. That racing car set didn't last long because the man (Mr. Augustus Walker or Duss as we called him) who put it together for me wore it out playing with it after putting it together.

I remember leaving the "BAT CAVE" on Christmas mornings meeting my buddies on the corner of Luther Street and Bells Mill Road. We would go from one house to another, seeing what each other got for Christmas. My cousins, Ovid Williams, George "Joe Joe" Moyler, Isaac Nichols, Anderson "Bro" Bell, Lamont "Ricky" Simmons, and Larry (Ricky's brother better known as "Sweetpea") were my partners in crime, not just on Christmas morning, but all through the year. These guys often came to the "BAT CAVE" to play (or get in trouble).

## LIVING IN THE BAT CAVE

I remember one year we had a terrible flood. The river located at the end of Luther Street was connected to the ditch behind our house, "BAT CAVE," overflowed. The water rose to the back porch. Our collie dog named Scott, who looked like the TV dog, Lassie, drowned during the flood. I guess Scott forgot to go to the dog's YDCA to take swimming lessons. Another dog that I had in my childhood was a dog I named King. King was a good dog, but like me, he loved chicken. The problem was he liked live chickens with the feathers on them. King would go down to Mrs. Elsie Small's chicken coop to make a selection for his paw licking good meal. Then, he would come back home with chicken feathers all in his mouth. Finally, my mom and my grandmother said that King had to go. So, for the love of chicken, I lost my dog—Memories, like the corners of my mind.

I remember the days going on the back porch to get some wood for the fire, and next door I could hear Mr. J.O. Alexander (Rev. James O. Alexander Sr. husband of Mrs. Sadie) playing his piano on his closed-in screened back porch. My mom would often say, "I wish Mr. James would get off that piano and go in the house." Playing the piano was one thing, but I could imagine seeing the angels cover their ears saying "PLEASE" when he would sing. I could hear them saying, "The Lord is in His Holy temple, let ALL the earth keep SILENT before Him." I loved Rev. J.O.

I remember at some point and time of life at 729 Luther Street. after Mama Creasy and Uncle Lloyd died, it was just my mom and myself. We rented out the upstairs rooms to a couple who had just gotten married. Betty Cuffee married Ruben (Bro) Griffin, and they moved in with us upstairs. I remember being so excited to have someone else in the house. I remember Bro painting the rooms upstairs. I remember going upstairs "all the time" to see them. They were my new friends, even though they were older than I was. I remember once my timing must have been bad. I heard Bro telling me, "Peterman, I think Mrs. Sweetie is calling you." I said, "Naw, she ain't." I didn't know, but now I understand. They did have two children, Calvin and Angela, while they lived with us, so I wasn't too interruptive. They later had another son named Lamont. I still see Bro and Betty at various church services. All these years, and they are still together. To God be the glory!

# 3.
# GREEDY BUTT

I called this chapter "GREEDY BUTT" simply because that is what I was, and sometimes I still fit that characteristic today. I shared with my wife and had her in tears (laughing) about my childhood food consumption. I always loved to eat, and it didn't make any difference where I was. I remember the cookouts in the backyard at the home of Mr. Cle and Mrs. Mary Bell who was also known as Ms. Bug. They always had cookouts in their large backyard serving hot dogs, hamburgers, and fried crabs! I remember Ms. Bug frying her good old' fried crabs in batter that was unbelievable. I mean ridiculously good! Ms. Bug also made homemade ice cream. I remember her fixing her homemade ice cream in a light blue barrel-looking ice cream maker. The ice cream was so good. Mr. Cle and Ms. Bug were very good friends with my mom, and they always invited my mom and me to come to their cookouts. I didn't want to disappoint them, so I felt obligated to go and make them feel good about inviting me. I would eat and eat and eat! There were two siblings, who shall remain nameless, who would walk back and forward along the back yard fence, hoping to be asked if they wanted something to eat. I had the nerve to say they were some "greedy kids," but now that I think about it, as a kid and perhaps even now, I've earned the title "Greedy Butt." So, there I was, eating and judging with my mouth full. The only difference between us was that they wanted to be at the cookout, but I was actually there, the absolute "Greedy Butt," eating.

Then, there were the Sunday dinners at the home of my great aunt Mrs. Cherry Durham (my grandmother's sister), and her daughter Cousin Pearl Holly. It would be a lonely evening around these grown people talking about stuff that I wasn't supposed to hear. Well, I rejoiced in the feasting part. Aunt Cherry and Cousin Pearl would cook so much food. I mean some good old soul food with high blood pressure seasonings. I definitely didn't want to make them feel like the food wasn't good, so I would eat, and eat, and eat. On a side note, I remember Aunt Cherry had a swing on her front porch similar to the one we had at 729 Luther Street. I remember how it was fun to sit on the swing hooked up to the ceiling and swing back and forth while looking at the cars going by. Aunt Cherry was on the swing one day when I was at her home. I was sitting on the iron rocking sofa, and, suddenly, I heard this loud bump as Aunt Cherry made a loud noise. The swing had fallen, and there was Aunt Cherry down on the floor, still sitting in the swing laughing. It was like Humpty Dumpty, who had a great fall.

Then there were those lonely evenings at the home of two of my favorite adults, whom I called Uncle Randolph and Aunt Mae Little. They were not really my relatives, but I loved them so much, and they were like best friends to my mom, so I've always called them Aunt and Uncle. So, anyway, here I find myself once more with adults listening to spirituals on their low volume radio while talking to each other with dim lights on. It was so boring, but I loved these people like they were my parents. Then, Aunt Mae would say, "OK y'all, it's time to eat." That's when everything would brighten up. Being there lonely was worth the sacrifice because I would eat, and eat, and eat and then eat some more.

I'm just a lover of food. I would eat when I was hungry, and I would eat when I wasn't hungry. Eating was fundamental. To this day, I believe eating is a serious business. For years, I wouldn't drink anything until I was finished eating. I didn't want to take up the space in my stomach reserved for food. I praise God for a cooking wife who knows what to do in a kitchen. It didn't take her long to find out that she would be married to a "GREEDY BUTT." She told me once that she could not believe my plate when she came to my house for the first time for dinner. I made a believer out of her. I was raised on Big Johnnie cookies (two for a penny), whiskey drop candy, Mary Jane candy, candy bars such as Paydays, Hollywood, Good Time, Hershey, Nehi Grape and orange sodas, potato chips, and chocolate chip cookies from Mr. Will's or Mr. Twine's or Mrs. Ruth's store. Mr. Will was Mr. William Alexander; Mr. Twine was Mr. Lonnie Twine, and Mrs. Ruth was Mrs. Ruth Massey. They all had their little grocery store in Bell Mill.

I remember lying on the ground as a young boy and looking up, imagining a big block of rice pudding the size of a house. I would picture myself eating in the doorways and the rooms. That's how much I loved rice pudding with no raisins. Even today, my two favorite dishes are grits and white rice with butter, pepper, and salt. At my Aunt Laura's house, I remember that there was always leftover breakfast on the stove in a bowl covered with aluminum foil. The cheese grits and bacon always had my name on it. For some reason, we hardly ever had leftovers at my house. I wonder why? I remember the taste of the old-fashioned hotdogs and hamburgers we had at the closing of the vacation bible school at the old Mt. Lebanon Baptist Church. There was something special about the mustard and relish and onions on those grilled hotdogs that you can't get today. Even the taste of the chicken from Kentucky Fried Chicken is not the same as it was back in the day.

I've been blessed, as I mentioned, with a wife, Teresa, who is the most gifted cook I know. There is nothing in her cooking that tastes bad. I mean, even if we eat out at a soul food restaurant, I'm usually disappointed because I expect the food to taste like hers. My absolute favorite, which I request every birthday or Father's Day, is her fried chicken or fried pork chops smothered in gravy. Can't "NOBODY" cooks like my baby Teresa. She loves to cook, and I love to eat, and that's why I titled this chapter "GREEDY BUTT."

# 4.

# GETTING MY "EDUMACATION"

My first school attendance was in kindergarten, which was held in the home of my kindergarten teacher, Mrs. (Ms.) Hattie Todd. For whatever reason, the folks in Bells Mill usually referred to her by calling her to always by her full name, "Hattie Todd." Her home was a two-story yellow and brown house just down the street from where I lived on Luther Street. Ms. Todd's house was located on Bells Mill Road next door to Ovid and Beverly's home. There is so much I remember about my kindergarten experience, including lunchtime. I can still smell the bologna and cheese sandwiches with mayonnaise wrapped in wax paper, resting in brown paper lunch bags that we carried for lunch. I remember the creepy stairs that curved with no handrails leading to the rooms upstairs, which we never attempted to investigate as nosey little children. Ms. Todd's grandson, Andrew Davis, was in my class and often told us that there was a ghost upstairs. Andrew was born about eighteen days before me, on August 29, 1955. He would become my lifetime friend until his death on September 25, 2006. Andrew was musically inclined, as was his family also and he played the bass guitar with great skill. Later in life, when I was the musician for a different church each Sunday, I would conduct

## THE THINGS I REMEMBER

mass concerts with all the choirs I played for. Andrew served as my bass guitar player.

I can still see the various magnetic alphabets; orange, yellow, red, blue, and green that we used on the magnetic board in kindergarten. It was in kindergarten that I learned the twenty-third Psalm. I don't remember our kindergarten graduation itself, but I remember the white robes and caps. I believe they were made by Mrs. Lillie Mae Bly, the sister of my future high school bus driver Mrs. Hattie Griffin. She was also the sister of one of my mentors in music, Mrs. Rosa Worlds.

I attended Bells Mill Elementary School from the 1st to the 6th grade. Research shows that Bells Mill Elementary was built in 1923 in the heart of the Bells Mill community. In 1943, a new school was built. This was the era of segregation, and while White children lived in Bells Mill (at or near the end of Bells Mill Road), only Black children attended the school. According to a dear elderly friend, Mr. Eldret (Dump) Watson, children from the community of Blackwater (specifically Head of River Road) and the communities of Long Ridge, Green Sea, and Fentress also attended Bells Mill Elementary. When Southeastern Elementary School was built in 1951, the children from these communities were rezoned to Southeastern. Back in those days, the central black neighborhood elementary schools in Chesapeake were Bells Mill (Bells Mill), Southeastern (Green Sea), Crestwood (Crestwood), and Central Elementary (Deep Creek). At Bells Mill Elementary in the the1961-62 school year, my first-grade teacher was Mrs. Sarah Gilchrist. She was a very special teacher to me. Mrs. Gilchrist attended Little Zion Baptist Church in the Oak Grove section of Chesapeake, where I served as the Minister of Music and later filled in three Sundays a month.

I remember the school building like it was yesterday. When you walked into the main doors, there was a hall to the right where 5th and 6th-grade classes, special education classes, the band room, and the library were. This hallway was part of the original school structure. It was accented by a dark framework, dark doors, and dark floor tiles built of older material. Upon walking through the main doors of the building, to the left was a newly built wing. There you had the light doors and the light floor tiles with the main office directly to the left and the combined cafeteria/auditorium straight ahead. The hall curved to the right where the first through the fourth-grade classes were located. I remember one day there was a terrible thunderstorm. The lightning struck the tall brick chimney at the far end of the "L" shaped building next to Alexander Lane. Dump, the gentleman mentioned earlier in this chapter, lived across from the school and still lives on the corner of Bells Mill Road and Alexander Lane today. However, the school has been torn down and replaced by single-family homes. The tall chimney of the school building stood across from the side of Dump's house. When the lightning struck the chimney, bricks fell onto Alexander Lane and into Dump's yard. According to my longtime friend William Holmes, residents of Alexander Lane, or "the school lane," as we used to call it, were not allowed to travel past the school. This was because large bricks from the chimney were knocked out of position. There was the danger that the chimney would fall down and injure or kill someone. In addition to the chimney, another staple of the Bells Mill Elementary school was the playground, including a full-sized basketball court. I remember the monkey bars, swings, sliding board, and the baseball field located in the distant part of the school's backyard. I can honestly say that the playground of Bells Mill Elementary School provided so much fun and entertainment for me as a kid growing up in Bells Mill.

As a student at Bells Mill Elementary School, starting from first through sixth grade, my teachers included Mrs. Gilchrist, Mrs. Winstead, Mrs. Mature, Mrs. Riddick, Mrs. Brown, and Mrs. McCoy. Mrs. McCoy, my former sixth-grade teacher, is an associate minister at Gordan's Chapel Africa Methodist Episcopal

Church in the Green Sea section of Chesapeake, VA. Our principal was Mr. J. James or, as we called him, "Pop James." Our school had only two buses that bused in children from other communities. At the end of the school day, I can still hear "Pop James" over the P.A. system announcing, "Bus 5 Dawson Town, Bus 5 Dawson Town." The other bus, Bus #4, transported the kids to and from Greenbriar Farms, Queen City, and Oak Grove.

In elementary school, I joined the school band with Mr. Ballard, our band teacher. I played the clarinet. Oh, how I remember the smell of Listerine in the band room because that was what we used to clean our instrument reeds. I remember the names of two buddies in the band with me, Rodney Ricks of Queen City, who played the trumpet, and Elliott Lawson of Greenbriar Farms, who played the drums. Both these communities still exist in the Greenbriar area of Chesapeake, Va.

My fifth-grade teacher, Mrs. Brown, had a ruler that she used to discipline (beat) us with. We used to sing a new arrangement of Diana Ross's song "Stop in the Name of Love" that said, "STOP IN THE NAME OF BROWN, BEFORE SHE SITS YOU DOWN, WITH A RULER, OOOH, HOOOH." Our custodian was an old white-haired gentleman by the name of Mr. Henry Manley. I remember the smell of the floor cleaner Mr. Henry used to sweep the floors, which appeared to be shavings of pencil erasers. I remember watching Mr. Henry pull out the folding tables and chairs on rolling carts from under the stage to transform the large room into either the auditorium or the lunchroom. I also remember being drafted to assist in this transformation on more than one occasion. During my stay at Bells Mill Elementary School, I remember sandwiches and soups served as lunch. I also remember the small cartons of milk and the ice cream sandwiches. During this time, a great friend of my mother's, who was just like a family member, Mrs. Matron Ivey, later to become Mrs. Matron Beckett, was the cafeteria manager. I remember her passing out the food and saying, "Here boy, take this and go sit down." She would give me two ice cream sandwiches. I was blessed and highly favored even back then. I remember our school nurse, Mrs. Quarles, whose husband was the greatest football coach ever at Crestwood High School.

On July 24, 2021, I was honored to preach the eulogy of my first-grade teacher Mrs. Sarah Gilchrist who passed away at age ninety-three. I showed the family and those in attendance the original diploma that my mother and I had saved since 1961-62. I read to those present what the diploma said concerning my successful completion of my first day in the first grade. I received an A in all categories, including behavior, observation, play, and group activity. The diploma was signed by Mrs. Sarah Gilchrist. I mentioned how proud I was to have been her "FAVORITE" student out of "all" that she had taught, which made the family and all others laugh. Then, I said that the most remarkable thing about the diploma wasn't just the fact that it was signed by Mrs. Gilchrist, but the most remarkable fact was that it was the first and only time in "ALL" my years of school that I made the honor roll. Boy, did that put out a laugh throughout the church!

We walked to school, and I remember the walks from Luther Street to Bells Mill Elementary. Just pass Mr. Charles Davis' house (Andrew's house), and Mr. "Big" Joe Davis' house was the railroad track. Sometimes we had to wait for the train to pass by. It ran from the Richmond Cedar Works sawmill to the concrete plant, located in Bells Mill. Many of the residents of Bells Mill migrated from North Carolina to Virginia to work at the mill or the concrete plant.

Upon graduating from Bells Mill Elementary School, I remember the song Mrs. Hodges, the school librarian, taught the departing 6th-grade class. The words go like this:

*Beyond the blue horizon*
*Waits a beautiful day.*
*Good-bye to you*

## THE THINGS I REMEMBER

*At Bells Mill School*
*Great opportunities await me.*
*I see a new horizon*
*My life has only begun*
*Beyond the blue horizon*
*Lies the rising sun.*

How the heck I remember that song, I'll never know. But one thing is for sure, leaving Bells Mill Elementary School opened up a whole new world for me. Watching Mrs. Hodges play the piano inspired me to want to play the piano.

Now, I was moving into a new world. I had lived in Bells Mill, played in Bells Mill, attended school in Bells Mill, and now I was venturing out to another world. You have to understand, going to the supermarket in Great Bridge, which was only about four or five miles away, was like going to Williamsburg, which was about fifty-six miles from Bells Mill. So, when going to Great Bridge, I was ready to pack my bags for a long ride out of town. Although Bells Mill had three or four convenience stores, two post offices, and three barbershops, it was exciting to travel to the "big market" in Great Bridge. It was like going on a trip.

Now, I'm about to leave Bells Mill Elementary School to attend Crestwood Junior High School. I was leaving the village I had spent my whole life to venture out into a new country about 6.3 miles from my house. I was thankful that I still had a loving home to return to at 729 Luther Street, owned by my Uncle Ovid initially' (Uncle Nick) mother, Mrs. Pearl Nichols (Cousin Pearl). Cousin Pearl met and married Mr. Alvin Tindell, and they lived on Bells Mill Road, just down the street from Luther Street. After the passing of Cousin Pearl, Mr. Tindell decided to sell the house to Mr. Pinky Dawson, and my mom and I had no choice but to move out of the "BAT CAVE" taking some memories with us and leaving many, many great memories behind.

## GETTING MY "EDUMACATION"

While I was in junior high school, Mom and I moved from 729 Luther Street to 937 Bells Mill Road which is about one quarter of a mile from each other. The house at 937 Bells Mill Road was originally owned by my Uncle Nick's father Mr. Edward (Ed) Bell but now belonged to my uncle. It was such a different life in junior high school. There were a lot more students and a different teacher for each subject. Also, instead of walking to school, now I found myself riding a school bus. We'll talk more about this move from 729 Luther Street to 937 Bells Mill Road in chapter thirteen, later in this book.

Living in Bells Mill was such a blessing in my life. I find that even in elementary school, God was preparing me for a life of music ministry. It seemed All I could think of was my church, The Mt. Lebanon Baptist Church, and my developing passion for gospel music, piano, and organ. When listening to the various Motown sounds on the radio, I could always identify the sound of the piano and the organ. While listening to and watching Mrs. Hodges, my elementary school librarian, play the piano at Bells Mill Elementary and while singing in Mt. Lebanon's #2 choir (under Mrs. Rosa Cuffee Worlds), I always listened for the music coming from their fingers. At my mother's church, The Lee's Chapel AME Church, I would do the same as I would hear my mother's first cousin, Mr. Sampson (Sambo) Moyler, playing the organ.

"Over my Head, I Hear Music in the Air."

# 5.

# A SILLY QUESTION

Have you ever had someone ask you a question knowing what your answer will be? I mean, if you give any other answer than the obvious right one, you know you're doomed. 99.9 percent of the beatings I got from my mom were given right before she asked me a dumb question. My mom would say to me after I had done something against her principles, "EDVARD, (she named me Edward), you don't mean to mind me, do you?" I mean, come on, what do you say? "No, mother, I don't mean to mind you," and then be crucified? Give me a break! This question from my mom's lips was always a prelude to the whipping of my life, which caused me to scream from a bass clef Bb to a treble clef C#.

I can remember my mom and grandmother telling me not to go back to the river ("back to the river," Bells Mill vernacular) at the end of our street, Luther Street. I was told not to play around the river for fear that I would fall in and drown because I could not swim. One of my best friends, Terry Davis, lived two houses from the river. He would go swimming all the time. I knew I would be crucified, buried, and not allowed to rise if I went back to the river with Terry. However, one day our neighbors, Mr. Hurly and Mrs. Rosa Satterfield (who had a lot of kids) took their children for a walk back to the river. I figured, "Surely if I went back to the river with them, it would be ok." So, I walked with them and was having a great time until I looked up the street and saw this image walking towards us. It was Mama Creasy walking with both hands behind her back. Her dress, which was shaped like a bell, was rocking from side to side. She came up to me and grabbed me by the risk. She put such a vice grip on me until I could hear the air leaving between her hand and my arm. It said "SSSSSIP." My grandmother pulled out a whip from behind her back with the other arm, and she whipped me all the way home. If that wasn't enough, she then reported this grand celebration of disobedience to my mother when she came home from work. I knew it was the beginning of my end. Well, when my mom, "Hurricane Sweetie," got home, my grandmother told her what happened, and then came that silly question. "Edvard, you been back to that river?" (She knew I had) "Didn't I tell you not to go back there?" (She knew she had) "You don't mean to mind me, do you?" (She knew I did). Then, it happened; pain, despair, and agony on me.

There was a big ditch behind our house, which was connected to that same river. The ditch ran some quarter of a mile from the river to Bells Mill Road and ran behind my house and other houses on the same side of my street. Sweetie had warned me not to play around with that ditch that had tiny tadpoles in it. Tadpoles are little baby frogs that we sometimes would catch by punching small holes in a tin can nailed to the end of a stick. Three houses down the street lived a lady named Mrs. Elsie Small. Back then, all adults could tell you what to do as if you were their child and you had to do it or get a whipping from them and another from your parents. So, to avoid cutting wood for Mrs. Elsie or doing any other chores she might want us to do, my friends and I (five of us) decided to walk along the ditch bank instead of the road. This ditch bank not only ran behind my house, but it also ran behind our neighbor's houses, Mr. (Rev.) James Alexander, Mrs. Emmaline Bell (the house now belongs to her grandson, Earl Bell), Mrs. Elsie Small, and Cousin

Pauline Bell (where my buddy Isaac lived). The idea was to end up near Bells Mill Road by traveling along the ditch bank, allowing us to come out next to Mrs. Minnie (Doll) Chesson's house. All went well until we got behind Cousin Pauline Bell's house with a fence along the ditch bank. As we walked along the ditch bank behind Cousin Pauline's, we had to hold on to the fence as we walked along side to side.

We only had about two feet of ditch shoulder to walk on, and as we walked, me being the heaviest and the last to walk, the ditch bank caved in, and into the big ditch, I went. As I mentioned before, there were little tadpoles in the ditch and the fellows joked that I had fish jumping out of my pockets. I was soaked and wet as I went home. You would know that the fellows followed me home, and as I got into the house, my mom says to me, "Edvard, you been in that ditch?" (She "knew" I had). Then came the question, "You don't mean to mine me, do you?" (She "knew" I did). "Take off them' wet clothes." I thought I had it made. She had never whipped me naked before. I thought she wanted me to put on some dry clothes so I wouldn't catch a cold. I thought she was concerned about my well-being. I thought I had avoided a whipping. She came out with that long white belt and began to anoint my body with pain. I knew the fellows were outside listening so I wouldn't cry. And then my mom said, "Oh, you're a man, huh? You ain't gonna cry? I'm gonna whip you 'til you cry!" I couldn't take it no' more. I began to respond with full volume as if I'd been touched by the spirit in church. And then my mama said, "Shut up that noise, I'm gonna whip you 'til you shut up!" Talk about being confused, I'm like, "Woman, make up your mind, 'PLEASE'!" I wasn't allowed to go out of the yard. When I went outside, the fellows asked me, "What was all that noise in there?" "I don't know. It must have been the television, "I responded.

Here's another thing I remember. I was telling my wife about a time when I was about twelve or thirteen years old. The clothing style in those days was the pinned striped, double vested, three-piece suits. My mom had always brought me hand-me-down clothes from the white folk she worked for. That was fine, but one day she came into some money. Sweetie bought me a black three-piece pinned striped suit, with a matching shirt and tie and a pair of "Mod Squad" sunglasses. Oh, man! I thought I was "HOT STUFF." That Sunday at our church, Mt. Lebanon Baptist, I stood out on the front steps and greeted "everybody" who came into the church. Peterman (me) had a brand new suit, and he wanted "everybody" to see it and know it! I didn't just think I was cute and cool, I "KNEW" I had it going on! You couldn't tell Peterman "Nothing" that day. I would have been a great usher in church that day because I spoke to "EVERYBODY" with a smile on my face. It's a good thing I didn't do no shouting back then because I would have told the spirit, "Oh no, not today, maybe next Sunday." I won't bout' to mess up my suit and lose my sunglasses on the floor and step on them and break them. I never got a new suit again until years later. Mr. Arthur White (husband of Mrs. Ornette White) bought me a new suit for the choir anniversary of our No. 2 Choir. I remember thinking I was hot stuff with that white dress coat and black pants with a blue or black shirt and a white bow tie. If I sang in that anniversary the way I looked, then I did some powerfully good singing. All the guys in the No. 2 Choir had gone to Fines Men's Shop for their clothing. Mr. Arthur White was such a blessing because my mom couldn't afford to purchase the uniform, we wore.

# 6.

# THE MIND IS A TERRIBLE THING TO WASTE

With all the technology in today's world, such as video games, YouTube, Instagram, Facebook, texting, very real-looking plastic guns, and rifles, little is left for the imagination. The kids in my day used their creativity. I mean, we made up stuff to do. Instead of model airplanes, we took sheets of paper and made an airplane. Instead of plastic guns and rifles that looked real, we took sticks and tree branches and pretended to have a gun. We'd pick out tree branches that had the "L" shape like a gun and combine the form with our vivid imaginations, it became a gun. We'd take a long tree branch, and it became a machine gun or a rifle. The sound of the gun or rifle came from our lips and mouths. We'd shoot at somebody with our stick guns and say, "I got you. You're dead." They'd say, "Naw, you missed." Then, we would shoot them again and say, "I got you now."

I remember as a little boy, all of us had a motorcycle. No, not a real one, but we would take a clothespin and pin a piece of cardboard in the spokes of our bikes. We would then listen to the noise as the cardboard hit against the spokes on the bike's tire. Then, as our imagination grew, we would tie balloons to the bike, allowing the balloon to strike against the spokes. It wasn't long before the balloon would burst, but it sure did sound good while it lasted. We had a great imagination back then to design our own toys.

Behind the home of Mr. and Mrs. Morris & Carol Etheridge, who lived next door to my Aunt Laura and Uncle Arthur's home, were about five piles or hills of dirt. My cousin Sarah (now Pastor Sarah Williams) would play house. The piles of dirt were all connected, so we would call one pile the kitchen, another pile the dining room, another pile the living room, and so on. We would run from one pile to another, announcing which room we were in. In our minds, we were really in a house. Now, that's a strong imagination. The mind is a terrible thing to waste.

Another toy we (the fellows) invented was called a twirly bird. We'd get a corn cob that the kernels had been removed from and stick a nail on one end of it. Then, we would go into the chicken house and get three or four feathers and stick them on the other end and throw it into the air. It would twirl around in the air going up, and because the nail weighed the front end down, it would come down. We had to watch out because it could hit you in the head. We made homemade go-karts, built bridges in the woods, tied coal bags on our backs, and became Batman and Superman. Man, you talkin' about some goofballs flying around and not being in the air. We would run and make the whistle sound that superman made when he would fly on the television program The Adventures of Superman with George Reeves as Superman. Our imaginations told us that we were really flying. I imagine the birds were looking down at us and saying, "Koo-Koo."

I remember being at my cousin Ovid's house. At night my cousins Ovid, Willis, Beverly, Lydia, Nadine, Diane, and Laura, or Lady as we called her, would take clothes hangers and straighten them out. Then, they would put S.O.S. pads on the end of them, light it with a match and swing the hanger around, watching the fire sparks leave the pads looking like fireworks. Then, there were the homemade go-karts at the home of my godfather Cousin George and Alwanza Moyler, where the fellows gathered to play almost every day. We would get the wheels off old lawnmowers or wheel barrels, find old two-by-four boards and make go-carts. Your engine was the person pushing you. Wherein some had high horsepower engines pushing, whoever I pushed usually had mule power instead of horsepower. I never was a fast runner unless, of course, I was being chased by a dog in the community or if it was dinner time. I would also run as fast as I could if I was running late getting home before dark when the Navy Yard bus came by at 5:30 pm. Mr. George Griffin (whose wife was my school bus driver on bus #84 from the seventh through the twelfth grade) was the "Big Blue" diesel bus owner that picked up and dropped off folk working at the navy yard. His evening runs through Bells Mill, dropping off navy yard workers around 5:30 pm, was the alarm clock for many of us to go home and look at the kid's show, *Bungles the Clown*. We knew when he came through it was time to head home or have hands laid on us in the name of our parents. And trust when I tell you, when hands were laid on us, we responded with the dance and shouting and speaking in an unknown tongue with tears running from our eyes. The things we did, we tried not to do anymore.

How can I ever forget driving the Honda motorbike belonging to my dear friend Andrew Davis! Randy Watson also had a motorbike. All the fellows felt that Andrew and Randy's parents were rich because no one else could afford to have a motorbike but them. Man, that was a lot of fun. They didn't need to use a balloon or cardboard for an engine noise because they had the real deal.

# 7.
# COME TO JESUS

I attended Mt. Lebanon Baptist Church as a young child. My mother was a member of Lee's Chapel AME Church in Bells Mill. As you can see, Lee's Chapel is a Methodist church, and Mt. Lebanon is a Baptist church. One may wonder how I managed to be in the Baptist church and not in the Methodist church with my mom. My mom and her baby brother Uncle Peco were members of Lee's Chapel with their mother and my grandmother, Mama Creasy. My Aunt Laura and Aunt Sugardoll were members of Mt. Lebanon Baptist. Their father and my grandfather, Papa John (who really didn't go to church), and his mother, great-grandma Sarah Little were members of Mt. Lebanon. As I mentioned before, my Uncle Lloyd was neutral, meaning he was a member of both churches by association. Being raised with my cousins Jackie, Verona, and Sarah in the same house, I followed them to Mt. Lebanon, and I became a member there.

I remember the Sunday school class with Mrs. Annie Mae Little (Aunt Mae) as our teacher. I really loved Aunt Mae, who really was not related to me but was like a second mother. When she talked, she sounded like Aunt Clara on the television sitcom "Bewitched." I remember the little Sunday school cards she passed out with the biblical pictures and our Sunday school lessons. I remember all the good times I had growing up in Mt. Lebanon Baptist Church. Memories of my favorite pastor of old, Rev. William Henry Sawyer, a resident of Portsmouth, Virginia, are especially dear to me.

I remember the night the congregation voted on Rev. Sawyer to be our new pastor. When the votes were counted, and Rev. Sawyer was elected the new pastor of Mt. Lebanon, I (at twelve years old) looked in the phone book and found his phone number. Rev. Sawyer often told how he received a phone call from a twelve-year-old boy. He said this twelve-year-old informed him that the congregation had chosen him to be the next pastor of the Mt. Lebanon Baptist Church. Rev. Sawyer told this story in July of 1987 when I preached my initial sermon to become a licensed minister of the gospel. I was young, but I loved my church, and I had a special love for Rev. William H. Sawyer. Although he had a full-time secular job, Rev. Sawyer was always working at the church. I would run down there whenever I saw his tan-colored Cadillac parked there. I loved my church. I remember once when there was a fire at the church in the winter with snow on the ground. My mom received a phone call telling us the church was on fire. I ran to my back porch at 937 Bells Mill Road, and I could see the red glare of the flames in the winter skies. My home was about three-quarters of a mile from the church. I ran down Bells Mill Road in the snow to the church. When I got there, Mr. Lorenzo Holley, a member who lived across the street from the church, was standing there looking. With tears in my eyes, I began to throw hands of snow into the flames because the Great Bridge fire department had not yet arrived. Praise God the damage was only in the back of the church, and because the wind was blowing the flames out and not in, our church was saved from more significant damage.

Well, the time came when I needed to meet and give my life to the Savior, our Lord Jesus the Christ. Back in those days, it seemed to me that the time to do this was during revival season. It took me three revivals to get "religion." My quest to "get religion" started, I believe, at Lee's Chapel, my mom's church. I sat on what was called the mourners' bench. The front pews were reserved for those seeking to "get religion." They had the fellows on one pew and the girls on the other. We would sit there and watch the preacher preach, not having a clue what he was talking about because we weren't listening. Then the saints (the old people) would come and gather around us, singing acapella and praying. I can see them now in my mind rocking from side to side with their "bad breaths" humming, singing:

*Come to Jesus, Come to Jesus*
*Come to Jesus just now, just now*
*Come to Jesus, Come to Jesus just now.*
*Then they would add all these verses:*
*He will save you and only trust Him and He is able*

Then there was the song:
*Is there anybody here*
*That love my Jesus*
*Anybody here that love my Lord,*
*I want to know,*
*I want to know,*
*Do you love my Lord!*

There were many other songs that were sung such as,
*Get right with God*
*And do it now*
*Get right with God*
*And he will show you how*
*Get right with God*

Another revival song was,
*This may be my last time*
*This may be my last time*
*This may be my last time*

## THE THINGS I REMEMBER

*Maybe my last time I don't know.*

Now, they would sing these songs over and over again. I remember Deacon Randolph Little (mentioned earlier) kneeling down and saying to me, "Son keep saying, Lord save my soul, Lord save my soul, Lord save My soul." I said it over and over and over, but I guess I wasn't saying it loud enough because nothing happened. Well, I looked over at the fellows peeping between my fingers, and I saw some of them jumping and screaming. People started clapping and saying, "Thank you, Jesus," as my friends were placed on another pew. I guess it must have been the pew for those who got it (religion). Well, I got up and started jumping and screaming as they did, then I felt the same exact grip on my wrist that I had felt when I went back to the river with the Satterfield family. It was Mama Creasy grabbing me and slamming me back down on the mourners' bench as she said, "Boy, you ain't got it yet." Man, I thought I had it. The revival lasted for a week, and I didn't get it. Well, next was the revival at Mt. Lebanon Baptist, where I attended with no success.

Finally, I went back the following year during the revival season to Lees Chapel. I finally "got it" and deposited my membership, not at Lee's Chapel with my mom but at Mt. Lebanon with my cousins. Years later, I learned that being saved did not require jumping and screaming but simply confessing with my mouth the Lord Jesus and believing in my heart that he was raised from the dead. That was when I really received salvation. After receiving salvation, I did begin to jump and scream because I have something to jump and scream about. I've been jumping and screaming ever since. Still, when I hear these songs today, it takes me back to the old saints who have gone to Glory now. I was honored to render music at some of the funeral services of these saints, where I played a medley of these old-time revival songs. All their singing around me and praying over me was just another way of saying to me, "Come to Jesus." So glad I came

When I am invited to preach, I often mention that my pastor, Pastor Sarah Eason Williams (my cousin), was once a "member of my church." As kids, we played church all the time in the hallway of the "BAT CAVE." Most of the time, we played alone, but sometimes we had other members such as Avis England (now Avis Hinton) and our first cousin Beverly Williams (now Beverly Jones).

We even ventured out, sometimes seeking a neighborhood revival crusade to play church with the Johnsons and at other homes. Man, I would preach, play the piano and organ, which was a 2x4 board on my lap, I would direct them singing, tell them when to shout and when to stop. I guess you could have called it "Rev. Peterman Ministries Inc." We had no idea that God was setting us up for a life working for him. Praise God, today, we all are deeply involved with various ministries of the Gospel. I had no clue that one day, my cousin Sarah would become my official pastor to my wife and myself and my daughter and her family. She was led to ordain me as the Pastor of Music and Media at our church. She ordained my wife, Teresa, to preach the Gospel and serve as our praise and worship leader. Pastor Sarah also licensed my daughter Sherita and her husband Raynald as youth ministers of our church. Still, my mind goes back to those glorious days of childhood playing church in the hallway as well as under the shade trees. The Bible says that we are to train up the child in the way he should go, and when he is old, he will not depart from it. We knew nothing but church, singing, shouting, praying, preaching, and yes, even fussing like church folks do today. There's nothing new under the sun. Even today, many are "still" playing church, yet God's grace and mercy endure forever. Jesus Christ is the same today, yesterday, and forevermore.

I am so glad that the true meaning of salvation was taught to me in my teenage years. I found out that it's not the shouting and knocking over pews that save you. I learned that the Word of God declares in John 3:7 in the words of Jesus, "Marvel not that I said unto thee, you must be born again." Then in Romans 10:9 in the Word of God tells us, "If we confess the Lord Jesus Christ and believe in our hearts that God has raised Him from the dead, we shall be saved." I thank God for His grace and mercy, which the Bible says endureth forever. I gave my life to Jesus. Haven't crossed every "T," nor have I dotted every "I," but I'm striving every day, pressing towards the mark, for the prize of the high calling in Jesus Christ. I must confess that God has been good and faithful to me. He has blessed me in so many ways. I've had many close calls on my job wherein I should not be here "but God." It's good to know that God looks beyond our faults and still supply our needs. Thank you, God, for your Son Jesus the Christ who died and rose again, that I might live a life of forgiveness and healing. I may not be what I ought to be but thank God I'm not what I used to be. Because He lives, I can face tomorrow because He lives all fear is gone. Now life is worth the living just because He lives.

# 8.
# ANSWERING THE CALL

II Timothy 4:2:
*Preach the word, be instant in season, reprove, rebuke, exhort with all long suffering and doctrine.*

Romans 10:14-15:
*…and how shall they hear without a preacher? And how shall they preach except they be sent? As it is written, how beautiful are the feet of them that preach the gospel of peace and bring glad tidings of good things!*

From my earliest years, I've had a desire to be a minister or a preacher. I feel it was and is a desire that the Spirit of God put in my heart, mind, body, and soul. As I've mentioned in this book, my cousin Sarah and I and our cousin Beverly, Avis, and others were always playing church. I remember Sarah and me being in the hallway of our home at 729 Luther Street on the staircase singing and shouting. I would put on my bathrobe and preach as Sarah pretended to be my congregation. At some point, Avis became a member of my church. Avis and Sarah were my choir members as well as my church members. I would tell them when to sing, when to shout and when to stop. When Sarah and I played church alone, she wanted to preach. I would say that she couldn't preach because she was a girl and females were not preachers. Boy, was God setting me up for a serious turnaround for the future. We carried our ministry to other houses under the shade tree. On Wednesdays, we would see and hear the adults in serious prayer meetings at various homes. My Aunt Laura (Sarah's mom), Mrs. Catharine Burton, Mrs. Mary Johnson, Mrs. Pauline Harris, Mrs. Evelyn Bazemore, Mrs. Lucille Hailes, Mr. Joseph Harris, and others could be heard singing and praying giving God praise with their hand claps and their tambourines. What an example they set for us young people concerning the seriousness of praying and praising God.

Growing older, that desire to preach stayed with me. When I started playing the piano and organ in my late teens, I got requests to be the guest speaker and youth speaker at different church services. I remember one of the first speaking engagements I received was to my mother's church, Lee's Chapel AME Church in Bells Mill. I was a student at Norfolk State College, which is now Norfolk State University. I can see myself in the pulpit with my white suit and a burgundy shirt with a white necktie. I had been asked by Mrs. Janet Batts (Ms. Alfreda) to be the youth speaker for an evening service. I also brought my gospel group from Norfolk State with me. Ms. Alfreda believed in allowing young people to be active in the church. I wasn't allowed to play the piano at my home church, Mt. Lebanon Baptist (the deacons thought I would get it out of tune). Ms. Alfreda would let me come to Lee's Chapel and exercise my gift as she cried for joy and would say, "Play baby."

By the time I was about twenty years old, I knew there was a call on my life to preach. I've heard many preachers confess that they "ran from the call to preach." I've even heard some say that God had to put them flat on their back with sickness until they answered the call. These things never happened to me. I can't say that I ran from the call, but my situation was in the form of a question. Was this just my desire to preach, or was it God's desire for me to preach? That was my struggle. I didn't want to preach to fulfill my desire. I wanted to preach because God called me to. I can remember being told by a preacher, "Go on and step out of faith." I was afraid if I stepped out on faith, I would be stepping out by myself. I needed to know that this was what the Spirit of God was calling me to do. I remember seeing up-and-coming preachers like Rev. Dwight Riddick, Rev. Michael Toliver, and Rev. James King aiming to become pastors. Somehow observing them in this capacity bothered me in my spirit because I felt I was being disobedient to the Spirit of God.

After I got married in 1978 (at the age of twenty-three), I still felt "this call" on my life to preach the Word of God. After my wife and I moved from Harbor North Apartments to a home on Fernwood Farms Road, I found myself having to drive past New Mt. Olive Baptist Church on Fernwood Farms Road. Each time I passed that church, I would look at it, and somehow, I felt in my spirit "some type of way" that God was calling me to preach. Then I would travel down Great Bridge Blvd. towards Battlefield Blvd. and take the ramp to the newly built Great Bridge By-pass (Rt 168). On my way to New Oak Grove Baptist Church, where I served as the church organist while approaching the bypass, I would see the back of the Little Zion Baptist Church. In the rear of the church, was and still is a big wooden cross. As I looked at the cross on the back of that church, I felt the same feeling in my spirit.

I had the nerve one day to pray to God and challenge him. I said to him in prayer, "Lord, if it is your will or desire for me to preach, please give me a sign." Well, guess what? There was an older lady at New Oak Grove Baptist church named Sis. Etheridge. We called her Aunt Reeny. In all the twenty-seven years I served there as minister of music, this lady never carried on a conversation with me. We would speak and give our God bless you and move on. Finally, one Sunday after church, she grabbed me by the arm and said to me, "Boy, I was in the field picking butter beans, and God told me you were going to preach." I laughed and said, "Yes, ma'am." She told me, "You don't believe me, do you?" I said, Yes, ma'am," not thinking about the challenge I had given to God. Sometime later, when I worked at a furniture store, a man I worked with, Mr. Warren L. Bryant, a supervisor there, called me Ed the Baptist. I asked him why he called me that. I figured it was because my name was Ed, and I belonged to a Baptist church. He told me that he called me that because I was going to become a preacher like John the Baptist one day. Then, in August 1984, with the assistance of Pastor O.L. Cromwell, II, pastor of New Oak Grove Baptist Church, I obtained employment as a mechanic with the Chesapeake Public Schools Transportation Department. This allowed me to see and experience the life of a preacher who was called by God. I was invited to speak at Bethel Baptist Church in Norfolk. I served as minister of music for the senior choir of Bethel, and Pastor Cromwell came to hear me. I still have a cassette tape of me preaching, and I can hear him responding to my preaching. Pastor Cromwell knew there was a calling on my life to preach, but he also knew it was up to me, and nobody else could accept that call. I watched him on the job as he ministered to the fellows. There were times when five or six of the fellows would come back to my working area, and he would be there. We would talk about God and his goodness. I would ask questions knowing that the guys were listening and hoping what they heard would be a blessing to them. It would become a joke with us when I would come to him and say, "I'm ready to preach." He would respond by saying, "Boy, you ain't ready, you ain't hitting on nothing." This went on for three years.

Finally, in 1987 I felt I couldn't live in peace until I answered the call that was on my life. God had already prepared my wife, Teresa. She knew that the call was there. A lot of people knew it, but I wasn't sure. When I told Teresa I was accepting the call to preach, she wasn't at all surprised. One day as I was driving down Fernwood Farms Road, passing New Mt. Olive Baptist Church,

I saw the pastor's white van parked at the church. Rev. Walter Mitchell was the pastor then, and I had great respect for him even though I really didn't know him personally. I felt led to stop by and talk with him about my calling. Rev. Mitchell knew me from playing at various services, and he took the time to share with me and pray for me.

I later found myself going to the home of Mrs. Evelyn Bazemore. She was one of those mothers of the church that was spirit-filled with the anointing. She would slap oil on you in a minute while speaking in tongues. If Mother Bazemore announced through prophecy that someone would have a baby, all the ladies would get scared and say, "Lord, is it I?" I told Mother Bazemore that I felt led to come and share with her that I felt the call to preach. She began to speak in tongues and took out the oil and anointed my head as she prayed. I remember her telling me to read in the Bible the 2nd chapter of Haggai.

I knew that telling Pastor Cromwell would only have him tell me in teasing, "Boy, you ain't ready," so I decided to contact the chairman of deacons at Mt. Lebanon Baptist Church, Deacon A.T. Alexander. By this time, Rev. William H. Sawyer, my favorite pastor at Mt. Lebanon Baptist, had retired from pastoring, and we were without a pastor. I informed Deacon A. T. Alexander of my call to preach. He was so happy but not surprised. He told me he would contact the other deacons of the church and set up the initial or trial sermon. Since we didn't have a pastor, he asked me if I could get someone to officiate over the service. Even though I wasn't a member of New Oak Grove, I really wanted Pastor Cromwell to be the one to sign my license. I didn't want to leave my home church, so this was a blessing. I told Deacon Alexander I had someone in mind. After getting things set up, I decided not to call Pastor Cromwell, but I walked around the corner to his home to share my answering the call to preach. We both lived in Fernwood Farms at the time. I rang the doorbell and sat down on the edge of his fireplace. I told him I was ready to accept the call. He said to me, "Boy, you're serious, aren't you?" I said, "Yes, I am." He slapped his hand on my shoulder and began to pray for me. Next, he began to mold me on the job (we worked together) by giving me written and reading assignments to complete. Finally, to top things off, one day, I was listening to Dr. Charles Stanley on the radio as I was breaking down tires. He was teaching about receiving and accepting the call to preach. Was that a coincidence? I don't think so. We set the date of my trial sermon for July 19, 1987, which was the third Sunday in July. It was a hot summer day in July when I nervously prepared to preach my initial or trial sermon.

While my wife was pregnant with our third child, she had surgery to remove a tumor weighing over ten pounds from around her uterus. The doctor didn't know for sure if it was cancer, so there were other specialists in the operating room. The surgery had been scheduled for later in the morning. However, the surgeon moved it up to earlier. I got a call about two hours before the move time. I rushed and got ready and went to pick up my Aunt Laura, who was like the medical personnel of our family. I had to backtrack to her house to pick her up, then travel from Bells Mill to Virginia Beach General Hospital in the Laskin Road area of Virginia Beach. This was about a thirty to forty-five-minute drive depending on the traffic. During that time, the Virginia Beach Expressway toll booths were up, so we didn't know if the traffic was backed up or not.

Speeding to Aunt Laura's home, I felt a voice speak to me while on Bells Mill Road. That voice said to me, "Slow down. God is with Teresa, and she is going to be alright. Take your time and don't have an accident." So, I slowed the car down, and when I got to Aunt Laura's home, she was running and rushing to get ready. I told her to slow down because everything was alright. It was raining that day, and it seemed to be the longest ride I had ever driven. When we got to the hospital, I immediately went to Teresa's room, and of course, she was not there. I looked out the big window that was located at the end of the hall near her room. It was raining both outdoors and in my heart. Aunt Laura and I went down to the waiting room where the surgery took place and waited for hours. I noticed that we were the only ones there but then sometime later, the waiting room was full. We waited, and we prayed.

I wished I could have arrived earlier just to tell Teresa that I loved her and assure her that everything would be alright. Hours later, after most of the other families had left, Dr. Phillip Turner came out with a serious look on his face. I had deep concerns for my wife's well-being. He was a man of small stature, so as I walked up to him and looked down into his eyes, he said to me, "What's wrong, Mr. Wilson? No need to be alarmed, your wife is doing fine." Oh my, what a relief it was to hear what I knew by faith was a fact! With great joy, Aunt Laura and I hugged and gave thanks to God. I wanted to see Teresa so bad. Aunt Laura said she would get something to eat at the cafeteria and asked if I wanted something. We were told that Teresa was in recovery and that we could see her in about an hour. As Aunt Laura walked to the cafeteria, I walked back up to Teresa's room. As I approached her room, I could see outside the big window at the end of the hall. It had stopped raining, and the sun was shining so bright. The trees looked as if they were made of glass. They were sparkling to the rays of the sunlight. Also, it had stopped raining in my spirit. I felt brand new, and my soul and spirit were sparkling to the rays of God's Son. That's when it hit me. God gave me a message for my trial or initial sermon. "HE SUN WILL SHINE AGAIN." A few days later, as I was going to a road call with my tire truck to work on a school bus, I received another confirmation. I remember I was on Campostella Road and Providence Road on a very cloudy day. The skies were a dark grey in color. Suddenly, the clouds separated, and I could see the beautiful light blue sky behind the dark clouds. Teresa's successful surgery and witnessing the light behind the dark clouds taught me

THE THINGS I REMEMBER

that "THE SUN WILL SHINE AGAIN." And it's all because of Almighty God's love, grace, and faithfulness.

I don't remember traveling to church on the Sunday of my initial sermon, nor do I remember being in the pastor's study before the service started. However, I remember how nervous I was when I walked into the pulpit and saw the church overflowing with people. Sister Rosa Worlds was at the organ with the #2 of Mt. Lebanon and the young adult choir of New Oak Grove Baptist Church. I remember them singing, "I'm saved, saved, saved by His power divine." I remember the pulpit being filled with preachers, including Pastor O.L. Cromwell II and my great father in the ministry, Rev. William H. Sawyer. Finally, after all the years of doubt, after all the years of feeling called to preach, and after all the years of prayer, the day had come. I felt as though a burden had been lifted off my emotional spirit of disobedience. When I really think about it, it wasn't that I was being disobedient, I was just being sure. I preached my trial sermon on the third Sunday of July 1987, but Pastor O. L. Cromwell II didn't license me until I preached at his church, New Oak Grove Baptist Church, on the third Sunday in August for their revival opening. From that point on until I left New Oak Grove some years later, I preached for the morning service on the third Sunday of August to open up their revival.

Over the years, I've been blessed by many individuals, including pastors, to preach at various churches. I have conducted revivals, preached funerals, and filled in for pastors who were on vacation. Rev. Jessie Arrington was the pastor of Bethel Baptist Church in Norfolk, Virginia, where I served as organist. He was also the pastor for Canaan Baptist Church in Suffolk, Virginia. Pastor Arrington served as the pastor of both churches for nearly forty years. Whenever he went on his summer vacation, he would allow me to preach at Bethel Baptist in Norfolk. I preached for their service at eleven o'clock. I then traveled down to Canaan Baptist in Suffolk, which started at one o'clock. Rev. Arrington was like a father to me. Another pastor I remember blessing me was Rev. Stanley Shepherd, the pastor of Little Zion Baptist in the Oak Grove section of Chesapeake, Virginia. He allowed me my first opportunity to commit the body to the ground of one of his deceased members. Mrs. Vandella Alexander, the wife of Deacon William Alexander. When the Rev. Anthony Moses became the pastor of Mt. Lebanon Baptist Church, he blessed me with a black ministerial robe trimmed in burgundy. Later, when Bishop Kim Brown became pastor of Mt. Lebanon Baptist Church, he blessed me with a collection volume of Henry Matthews Commentary books. I have been truly blessed by God through these preachers of the gospel.

God has truly blessed me to have many inspiring preachers and pastors in my life, such as Rev. William H. Sawyer, Bishop O.L. Cromwell II, Dr. Michael Toliver, Dr. William Chatman, Dr. Jessie Arrington, Dr. Anderson Foreman, Bishop Kim W. Brown, Pastor Tyron Johnson, Bishop Anthony Rodgers, Pastor Horace Cross, Bishop Daryl McCleary, Pastor Keith McPherson, Pastor Kevin McDonald, Bishop I. Joseph Williams, and last but not least my pastor today, my cousin Dr. Sarah E. Williams. Of course, I know a lot of preachers and pastors, but these folks had a significant influence on my life.

*A charge to keep I have*
*A god to glorify*
*Who gave His son my soul to save*
*And fit it for the sky.*

*To serve the present age*
*My calling to fulfill*
*O may it all my pow'rs engage*
*To do my Master's will.*

# 9.

# HUMOR IN THE FAMILY

There have been several funny situations that came up in our family in times of sorrow. Let me, first of all, tell you how I learned my mother's real name All my life, I knew that my mom's name was Mrs. Alberta Wilson. My mom had a nickname called Sweetie. Well, everybody called her Mrs. Sweetie. All her siblings had these nicknames like Sweetie, Nin, Sugardoll, Baby, and Peco. One day my cousins Jackie, Sarah, and Rona took their mother, my Aunt Laura, to Richmond to get her birth certificate in Richmond, Virginia. They also had to find some legal papers on my mom to get the information for Aunt Laura or Nin. I got this phone call from them informing me that my mom's first name was not Alberta. "What!" I responded. My cousins discovered, from state records, that my mom's actual name was Sweetie Alberta Wilson. I went to her bedroom in my house and said to her, your first name is really Sweetie and not Alberta. She told me, her only begotten son, who thought he knew what his mother's name was, "I know that." I said to her, "I'm so glad you decided to tell your son what your real name is."

Our family had a trademark of being highly emotional at the time of death in the family. I can recall my mom on the phone when someone had passed away. She would get a call about the death of a loved one and then call back for confirmation saying, "Is it true?" Then I would hear that voice of sorrow saying, "Oh Lord, Lord have mercy, umph, umph, umph, Lord have mercy." Then many, many phone calls would be made spreading the word of the passing of a loved one. My mom would call different ones and tell them of the unfortunate death, and before they could say "goodbye" or "I'll talk to you later, Sweetie," they would hear a click, and she was gone! The phone receiver would touch the tone button and jump right back to her ear for the next phone call to be made.

My mom was the funeral supporter of Tidewater. If there was a funeral and she could get a ride, she was there. I recall when Deacon Turner, a deacon at New Oak Grove Baptist Church in the Blackwater section of Virginia Beach, passed away. I was at the organ. Mind you now, my mother did not know this man but insisted on going with me to the funeral I had to play for. So, I'm at the organ playing when I hear this familiar voice in the congregation crying out loudly, declaring, "I'm gonna miss that smile." Yes, it was a woman who didn't know the man with a great smile. This woman I called mom.

One of the ministers in our family was named Rev. Joseph Durham, better known to us as Cousin Jody. I don't mean to be disrespectful, but our cousin was known to be a member of the gay community. I guess we should have called him Cousin Judy (just kidding). I loved Cousin Jody, and when he passed away, his body was brought back from New York to his hometown of Bells Mill. I was asked to serve as a pallbearer for his funeral. With me was my Cousin Rodney Creekmore, my mother's first cousin. Cousin Rodney was a short, small statue of a man who would always make you laugh. Going into the church, I had the front part of the casket where all the weight was. Cousin Judy (I mean Jody) was a large man. After the funeral, we took the casket out and put it in the hearse. I started back towards the church to make sure my family was ok as they came out of the church. Cousin Pearl

HUMOR IN THE FAMILY

Holley came out with her handkerchief to her face, crying, "Jody, Lord Jody, Lord have mercy, Jody." As I watched Cousin Pearl approach the steps to come down the walkway, I saw her peeping through her fingers to make sure she didn't miss a step as she was walking down the steps screaming uncontrollably. All I could do was smile, holding back my laughter. When we got to the cemetery, the way we lined up at the hearse, I managed to be at the foot of the casket where there was less weight. Cousin Rodney, unexpectedly, ended up with the front of the casket where the weight was. Cousin Rodney was small and sought of short man and being at the front of the casket worked to his disadvantage. Mr. Fitchett, the funeral director was walking in front of the casket as we carried it to the grave, which was about twenty or thirty yards from the hearse. Mr. Fitchett was walking ahead of the casket as we followed. He was saying as we walked past and over other graves, "Go over to your left fellows, ok now walk to your right," which prevented us from stepping on other graves. By this time, the rain began to lightly fall. Cousin Rodney, who I could tell had had a little nip before the funeral, said to Mr. Fitchett, speaking loudly "Shut up, man and help us. This nigger is heavy." If I didn't know any better, I would have declared that I heard Cousin Jody laughing with us. Mr. Fitchett just kept walking.

Then there was the funeral for my cousin Irvin Eason. Irvin was one of the sons of my mother's sister, Aunt Laura, and he was the brother of my cousins Jackie, Rona, and Pastor Sarah. There were three other brothers, Gene, Don, and Eddie. Irvin had lived in New York and had spent many nights and a lot of time up there with Uncle Nick and Aunt Sugardoll (Aunt Laura and my mom's sister and brother-in-law). Irvin died of cancer, and his funeral was held in Lee's Chapel Church in Bells Mill. When the time came to view the body, I took my usual place beside the casket with the undertakers because I knew my family's history of emotional expressions. Aunt Sugardoll came around to view the body, and her hands went up in the air! She was crying, "Irvin, Lord, have mercy, Irvin, Lord, Irvin!" As I approached her, she put her handkerchief to her face crying. I was escorting her to her seat (which was the wrong seat) when right in the middle of her crying, a non-crying voice said to me, "Edward, I was sitting over there" then the crying continued.

    I don't mean to take the feeling of grief from my family lightly. I, too, have had moments wherein I lost control. I recall when Uncle Arthur Eason passed away. This was my Aunt Laura's Husband. The only daddy I knew coming up as a little boy. I used to call him Dad probably because Sarah and Rona were so close to me in age, and they were his children, and I called him what they called him, but also because he was the male role model I had in my life. He was like a father to me. At his funeral in 1980, I remember trying my best to control my emotions. But, when I went to view his remains, I just lost it and ran to the back of the church and cried all the tears I had held back since his passing. So, I understand and respect the emotional expressions, yet I find some laughter in some of them.

    When my mom passed away, the funeral was just as she had requested. My lovely, sweet wife Tesee took care of the details of dressing Sweetie. We got Cousin Velda to do her hair. Tesee picked out the beautiful dress and earrings my mom wore. Sweetie had on a white hat and white dress. Tesee did a GREAT job! I remember when we went to the funeral to view Sweetie to ensure all was as we wanted. As I looked at my mother, she was so beautiful. She looked like she was naturally sleeping in a church service. My cousin Velda had done a beautiful job with Sweetie's hair. It was so pretty. I remember taking my finger and rubbing back her hair so the pretty earring could be seen. My mom loved jewelry. She had on white gloves with rings on them. Sweetie looked like she was going to meet my dad for a prom date in heaven. She was so pretty I honestly couldn't cry. At the funeral, I remember the church being packed to its capacity. I remember walking in the church, and feelings of physical hurt but spiritual satisfaction hit me. The service was truly a homegoing, and it was as she had desired it to be. She had requested in writing that her body would remain in the front of the church during the viewing. It was the custom of many families to view the remains at the back of the church. We once joked about it. I asked her if I didn't put her up front but took her to the back of the church for viewing, what would she do about it. She said to me, her only begotten son, "If you do, I'll come back and haunt the s... out of you." I knew at her funeral that wouldn't happen, but I wasn't about to take any chances. She was viewed at the front of the church. Walking out the church behind her casket, following the hearse to the gravesite, seeing the top of Sweetie's casket through the back window of the hearse all brought me to tears. As we left the cemetery with her casket still above the ground over her grave, I thought about that being the one thing that was most sad to her. She always talked about the sadness of leaving the cemetery with the casket of our loved ones still in view resting over the grave. The good news was and is that only her remains were left in the casket. She had flown away a few days earlier, going to sleep in our house and waking up in God's house. To be absent from the body is to be present with the Lord.

Ok, so much for the serious stuff. Let me give just one more example of comedy in a sorrowful situation. When my Aunt Laura, my mother's sister, passed away, the homegoing service was held at the Chapel of The Mount (Mt. Lebanon Baptist Church), which is located behind what used to be our baseball field. Aunt Laura had made the same request as my mom, that she wanted her remains to be viewed at the front of the church. However, Mr. Carlos Howard, the funeral director, told the family to remain seated, and he had his people roll Aunt Laura's remains out of the sanctuary. We thought they were putting the body in the hearse. My mom was in a wheelchair. I decided to take her out of the sanctuary ahead of the rest of the family to avoid holding up everyone else leaving the church. My mom never wanted the footrest down on her wheelchair. She would just hold her feet up when she was being rolled around. My son-in-law Monzie and I were taking her to the limousine. When we turned the curve to head for the door, there was Aunt Laura laid out in the vestibule to be viewed. Monzie tried to push Sweetie to the door, but she put those feet down like Fred Flintstone in his car. The wheelchair came to a halt, and with her feet, she turned the wheelchair in the direction of the casket while screaming, "Lord Laura." With her feet, she rolled the wheelchair up to the casket and stood up to see Aunt Laura. She pulled on the casket to get up from the wheelchair, and I was afraid she would tilt the casket over and pull Aunt Laura out, so I pulled her down to the wheelchair. Monzie looked at me with those big eyes as if to say, "What the hell do we do now?" My son-in-law declares that I slammed her down, but I don't recall that. All I know is there was power in Sweetie's knees and legs and feet that day. I always said I could write a book on our family that would be a best seller. I praise God for my family and the humor that we bring in life.

I remember cousin Lavern Eason, the daughter of Don and the granddaughter of Aunt Laura and Uncle Arthur, telling us about an experience she had while living in New York City. She told us that she got on the elevator one day and was about to go up several stories to a friend's apartment. After she got on the elevator alone, about three or four Puerto Ricans got on the elevator with her. She became frightened that they would rob her or attack her in some way. Some brothers (black men) got on the elevator a few floors up, and she now felt safe. Guess what happened. When the elevator stopped at the next floor, and the Puerto Ricans got off, and after the doors closed the brothers robbed her.

# 10.

# MRS. SWEETIE

My mother, Mrs. Alberta (Sweetie) Wilson, was born on August 1, 1911, in South Mills, North Carolina, to my grandparents Mr. John Williams and Mrs. Creasy Roberts Williams. My mom lived with my wife and me for over twenty-five years until she passed away. One day about two years before my mom went home to be with the Lord, she called me on my house phone. I was home in bed sick, but my mom didn't know I was home. She called my job and asked for me, and my supervisor, who loved her, told her I was probably in the next room near her room sleeping because I was sick. Sweetie called my phone from her bedroom, and we talked for over an hour. I wish I had recorded the conversation because she gave me her complete biography from when she was born to the present time.

    At an early age, around twelve or thirteen, living in South Mills, North Carolina, she saw her father, my grandfather Papa John with another woman. She never told my grandmother Mama Creasy. Somehow Mama Creasy found out about his affairs, and she approached him about them. Papa John assumed that my mom Sweetie had told Mama Creasy about it. So, he put my mom out of the house. Sweetie was put on a train and rode up to Virginia to the

Fentress train station, where she was picked up by Mama Creasy's sister and brother-in-law Hosea and Cherry Durham.

She stayed with Aunt Cherry and Uncle Hosea for a good while, then she moved in with Mama Creasy's other sister, Aunt Sarah Creekmore. Sweetie said she alternated from house to house. Both of these houses are located in Bells Mill, and both still stand. Finally, she moved to New York with Aunt Mary Woodard, another sister of Momma Creasy. My mom's sister, Aunt Sarah (Sugardoll) Nichols, married Uncle Ovid (Nick) Nichols a few years later. My mom lived with them for a while, and she met a man named Cornelius Wilson. At the early age of, I think, sixteen or seventeen, she married Mr. Cornelius Wilson, who already had a son, perhaps from a previous marriage, named Benjamin Wilson. Mr. Cornelius was in the navy, and my mom said that the first couple of years were good years. Then Mr. Cornelius began to drink heavily and began to physically abuse my mom. He would come home to a neatly cleaned home and hit my mom because the refrigerator had stopped working. Sometimes Mr. Cornelius would get home late and would beat her because the dinner had gotten cold. This went on for years until one day, Mr. Cornelius's son Benjamin fought him over my mom because he loved her like she was his own mom. She was once put in the hospital for nearly a year because of his abuse. Finally, his relatives, who loved my mom, came to their apartment while Mr. Cornelius was at work, packed her bags, and moved her from New York back down to Virginia.

Uncle Arthur, the husband of my mom's sister Laura, worked at Royster's Fertilizer Co. off Bainbridge Blvd. in South Norfolk. He had a fellow worker there that he was friends with named Edward Marvin Ashby. Mr. Ashby would come out to Bells Mill with my uncle to visit. He met my mom, and they fell in love. As a result of them communing together physically, I was produced. As my mom once told me, "I was an accident." I told her I was the best accident she had ever had. My mom was my mother and my father.

She taught me how to tie a necktie and how to wear men's cologne. She taught me to be a respectful, peaceful man and not a violent man because of what she had been through with her husband.

I am my mom's only child, born when she was forty-four years old. Sweetie is one who loved everybody, and I really do believe that everybody loved her. I lived in her home for twenty-three years until I got married. She lived in my home for twenty-five years until she moved in with Jesus. I praise God for a beautiful, loving mom.

## 11.

# THE TIE THAT BINDS

I thank God for my family. My mom Sweetie, Aunt Laura, Uncle Arthur, Aunt Sugardoll, Uncle Ovid, Uncle Lloyd, Uncle Peco, and Aunt Mary, and of course, and my loving Grandmother, Mama Creasy.

**MAMA CREASY** was my dearly loved grandmother whose full name was Creasy Roberts Williams and was better known to her grandchildren as Mama Creasy. Mama Creasy was a tall slim woman with pretty, grey hair, which I remember there being a tint of blue in her hair. Her hair was usually laid down and curled at the end. I can see Mama Creasy's soft, smooth, wrinkled skin. She wore kitty cat eyeglasses. Her dresses seemed to be starched in the shape of a bell. Many nights, as a family, we gathered in the dining room, which held a cot that Mama Creasy used as a bed, to watch the little black & white television. Her favorite TV shows were Gunsmoke, The Big Valley, Lawrence Welch, and the wrestling match with George Baker, Johnnie Weaver, and Haystack Calhoun as her favorites.

Sometimes she would fall asleep, and I would sneak up, grab the pliers, and softly turn the channel. Then, she would wake and holler, "Turn it right back. I was just resting my eyes." I wanted

# THE THINGS I REMEMBER

so bad to tell her that she should have rested the snoring while resting her eyes. Mama Creasy was an usher at Lee's Chapel AME Church. I can see her now standing at the door with a church fan in her hand, collecting chewing gum from the mouth of those of us who had the nerve to chew gum in God's house. That, evidently, was a sin before God, and she was the sin preventer. I never understood why we couldn't chew gum in church, but Mama Creasy and her sister Aunt Sarah Moyler Creekmore could dip snuff. The snuff was called "Square Snuff." I can see it now in the little round red can. I can also see the empty tin can she used to spit out the chewed-up snuff. Nasty enough to spoil "MY" appetite. Now, you know that's nasty.

When Mama Creasy watched her westerns like Gunsmoke, Rawhide, and The Big Valley, she couldn't understand how it could be night in one scene and daytime after the commercial break. I can hear her now saying, "How in the world it git' day time so quick?" I remember in her last days, my grandmother lived with my Aunt Laura. I remember the hospital bed in the living room. I remember when we got the word that Mama Creasy had passed away at the age of seventy-three. It was April 23, 1967, I remember walking into Aunt Laura's house after school, and the hospital bed was empty. So was my heart. I had lived with my grandmother all my life. Can't remember when she moved in with us at 729 Luther Street because, in my mind, I see her always being there. I remember her telling me to get some corn remover and put it on her toes. She always said that I was going to be a foot doctor when I grew up. Mama Creasy was buried just about fifty yards or less from our home known as the "BATCAVE" and just a few feet from where she would cut off those wet inside switches, which she used to show love and care for my future. When a concrete slab was built over her grave, you can still see my fingerprints where I wrote her name, birth date, and date of death with my ugly handwriting. At her funeral, when I was about twelve years old, the one song I remember hearing was "It is well with my soul." I would go out to her grave every day and sing that song to her until I figured she wasn't there, plus I got tired of going in the cemetery singing to dead flowers. I was the only grandchild out of fifteen who lived with this godly woman every day. I had, and have, no doubt that she is where I plan to be, in the arms of Jesus the Christ resting from her labor.

I miss you, Mama Creasy. I wish you could be here to see three of your grandchildren preaching the word of God. You used to always enjoy the lady on Lawrence Welch named Joann playing the piano. I wish you could be here to hear your grandson praising God on the piano and on the organ. I wish you could see your great and great-great-grandchildren today as they hear about this woman so dear to us known as Mama Creasy. I wish I could remember your husband, my grandfather, Papa John. I remember the name, I remember the shack on the riverbank where he stayed, but I just can't picture my grandfather, Papa John. I wish that I could remember his face. But there are things I remember about Mama Creasy. Mama Creasy, I remember the smell of your clothes fresh off the clothesline. I remember the dream I had about you that took place in the old Lee's Chapel AME church that seemed so real. I walked into the sanctuary from an outside color vision to an inside black and white image. I talked to you as you smiled. You never said a word, but you carried a shopping bag with something in it that I could not see. You got up and waved with a smile and walked down the aisle towards the pulpit. As I exited the church, I walked back into a color vision. I remember you telling Sweetie when I was hard-headed and didn't mind you. Then you got mad with her when she beat me. I hear you saying, "Sweetie, don't beat the boy." You were so precious to me. You were my grandmother, and you were my friend. I love you, Mama Creasy, and will forever carry you in my heart. Your song:

# THE THINGS I REMEMBER

*When peace like a river*
*Attendeth my way*
*When sorrows like sea billows roll*
*Whatever my lot Thou has taught me to say*
*It is well; it is well with my soul*

It was well with your soul Mama Creasy so rest in peace. You fought a good fight, you finished the course, and you kept the faith. Well done!

**AUNT LAURA** was always like a second mother to me. She was my spiritual mentor. I can see her now holding down the back of her dress while skipping and dancing for the Lord as only she could do. She was the doctor of the Bells Mill Village. When folk got sick, they called on Mrs. Laura, who was a nurse. When folk died, the family would call on Mrs. Laura. She has closed many eyes of folk who took their flight to glory, leaving an empty, open-eyed shell. She was a praying, bible reading, and spirit-filled woman. I can see her now in church and in her kitchen praising God. She would grab her dress like she was about to sit down, and she would declare in her spiritual language, "Hi-Yah." Then, she would proceed to dance in the spirit with a smile on her face while rocking back and forward. Her name for my wife was "Precious." I was simply Peter. I remember going to her house at 932A Aberdeen Lane, where she always had breakfast leftovers. My favorite was her cheese grits and her homemade buttered rolls. She passed away on June 20, 2005.

**AUNT SUGARDOLL** lived in New York at 665 Westchester Ave. in the St. Mary's apartment project houses. There were three or four twenty-one-floor buildings in New York. Aunt Sugardoll and Uncle Nick live on the tenth floor. I remember waking up at 729 Luther St. to the noise of laughter, and I could smell the smell of

Aunt Sugardoll's perfume (Estee Laude). I knew then that she and Uncle Nick were home. Then, I would see the green suitcases. I was excited when Aunt Sugardoll came home because I knew I would be able to stay up later to watch television while she and my mom were talking about any and everything. Besides that, Aunt Sugardoll would always give me some money to buy cookies and candy with. Aunt Sugardoll always talked "proper" dialogue, but when she got juiced up from nipping, that's when she would really talk proper. I can see her now walking on her tiptoes and pointing her finger while saying, "Edward, as my mother used to say." Then she would tell me some "saying" that Mama Creasy used to say. Aunt Sugardoll used to call my mom Heedy. She lived in New York some forty years plus before she and Uncle Nick moved back to Bells Mill after they retired. At one point, we had many, many relatives in New York, but they are all gone now. Aunt Sugardoll passed away on March 17, 2002. I consider myself blessed to be the son of Sweetie, the grandson of Creasy, and the nephew of Laura, Sugardoll, Arthur, and Nick.

**UNCLE ARTHUR** was the husband of my Aunt Laura. Because he was missing a few fingers due to an accident on his job, he earned the nickname "Nubby." I remember Uncle Arthur always sweating and using his handkerchief to wipe his face. I remember the big bowl he drank coffee out of. I remember him always under the trees on the side of his home at 932A Aberdeen Lane, working on his lawnmower. I remember being with him when he would put gas in the car, and he would ask for two dollars' worth of "regular." I recall Uncle Arthur coming to our home at 937 Bells Mill Road and he would keep harassing my mom, joking with her asking her, "Sweetie, why are you so fat." My mom would say, "Go on Arthur, I ain't messing with you." Uncle Arthur would keep on joking with mom until she would get fed up and curse him out. Then, he would laugh with satisfaction and go on home. When Uncle Arthur died in 1980, two years after Teresa and I were married, I lost it at his funeral and ran in the back. This man, who was the only dad I knew, was gone. As a child, I used to call him dad. Perhaps, I called him dad because my cousins Sarah, Rona, and Jackie called him Dad. Maybe I called him Dad because, in my mind, he was my dad, and he was teaching me how to be a mechanic. I loved my Uncle Arthur, or as some called him, Shorty or Nubby. He passed away on August 13, 1980.

**UNCLE LLOYD** was better known by his siblings as "Baby." He was one of my mom's younger brothers. Uncle Lloyd was a good-looking, pretty, wavy-haired man who always had a toothpick in his mouth. To this day, I love to put sugar in my beans because of Uncle Lloyd. Uncle Lloyd wasn't churchy at all. He worked at the Richmond Cedar Works in Bells Mill and worked for our family friend Mr. Cle Bell running his candy store and his dance hall wherein the fellows would come and sit at a booth and get a fifty-cent shot (booze). I was always sure to get some candy and cookies for free from my Uncle Lloyd. On a Christmas Eve night, I remember walking down Bells Mill Road as a young boy, maybe about six or seven years old, holding Uncle Lloyds hand. I didn't realize that it was the night that Santa Clause was to come until he told me, "I've got to get you home because Santa is coming tonight." I got so excited and began pulling his hand as if I was walking him home instead of him walking me home. I really loved my Uncle Lloyd. I remember when he died, it was said that his favorite song was "Peace in the Valley." I pray that Uncle Lloyd found that peace when he left us and traveled to eternity. He passed away on October 7, 1966.

**UNCLE WILLIS** or Uncle Peco was the baby of all my mom's siblings. He was the father of Willis Jr., Ovid, Laura, Lydia, Diane, Beverly, and Nadine. Uncle Peco was tall with big eyes. I recall when he built his home, now occupied by his daughter Beverly and Ronnie, her husband. This was at the time one of the prettiest homes in Bells Mill. It still looks good today. When Uncle Peco built a separate garage in the back, I was young and told my mom to pack me lunch because I had to work with Uncle Peco. His home and garage were and remain today, located on the corner of Bells Mill Road and Luther Street, 900 Bells Mill Road, just across the street from Mr. Cle Bell's home and five houses away from our house at 729 Luther St. on the other side of the street.

When I arrived to work where Uncle Peco was building the garage that I was supposed to be assisting him with, I would eat my lunch as soon as I got there and then tell Uncle Peco that I had to go home. My workday was over, and he never fired me. Also, I need to let you know that he never paid me for "some" reason. I wonder why? I remember Uncle Peco singing in the senior choir at Lee's Chapel AME Church. I can hear him leading a song, "Nobody's Fault But Mine." I remember the verse, "If I don't make it to heaven, it will be nobody's fault but mine." He passed away on August 27, 1966.

**UNCLE NICK,** whose name is Ovid, was my Aunt Sugardoll's husband and is who I referred to as my rich uncle. That is because when I was a little boy, he would drive down from New York in a different car each time he came I didn't know that he didn't even own a car at the time. All I knew was my uncle and my aunt from New York came down in a different vehicle each time, and they looked rich and smelled good. They also gave me money and brought me gifts. That's what I call "rich relatives." Well, I found out later in life that Uncle Nick leased cars all the time and never owned a car until he was about to retire and move back down south. He didn't need to own a car because he worked with the New York Transit System and all this traveling within the system was free. Uncle Nick was always neat in his appearance and had a diction like no other. He talked like one from up north and was a very smart man. He told me that he attended the march on Washington with Dr. Martin Luther King Jr., and he was a friend of Congressman Adam Clayton Powell through our cousin Judge Howard (Bugzy) Bell. I loved Uncle Nick and considered him to be a father from afar. I always said when I saw Uncle Nick in his younger years that he looked like Sidney Poitier. Whenever I had a need, I could always depend on Uncle Nick to help me out. My greatest joy was listening to him, and Aunt Sugardoll "get" into it about things in their past lives. It was fun hearing Uncle Nick say like nobody else could "SUGARDOLL, PUN-KIN," and hearing Aunt Sugardoll say to Uncle Nick, "Shut up ORVID." Uncle Nick passed away on March 18, 2009.

**EDWARD MARVIN ASHBY** is the name of my biological father. My dad's presence in my life can be likened to that of a visiting relative who showed up periodically to maintain a romantic relationship with my mom. I loved my dad, but I only wish I could have had a father-son relationship with him. There are only a few times I can recall him giving me a few dollars for gas which lets you know that I only knew him in my late teens. The memory of my dad is that he was a quiet man with a giggled laugh. The only time you knew he was present was when he had been drinking. I often wondered what caused my dad to drink as he did. I remember most of the time when I saw him, he was intoxicated. When he wasn't drinking, he was so quiet and sweet. When he was drunk, he just fussed all the time. One night, I got so upset with him because of how he had talked to my mother I put him out of the house. It was a snowy cold night. It wasn't long I was out looking for him. I found him and brought him home. I took off his pants and laid him on the couch in the living room. In talking to my sister Caroline, I learned that our dad wasn't a drinker until one night he had an argument with her mom Mrs. Mary. Caroline said she was a little girl, but she remembered seeing our dad choking her mom with a broom. Don't know what the argument was about, but she had never seen him like that. He wasn't a violent man. The next thing she knew, her mom had her and our younger siblings packed up and walked from their home in Campostella at three in the morning to the house of the elderly couple that she was a caretaker for in the Berkley section of Norfolk. My mom told me that my father was always a clean, neat man who always had money. I often wonder if that situation of conflict with Mrs. Mary Cuffee drove him to drink. I wonder whether this was when Mrs. Mary found out that my dad had another child out in Chesapeake. He was never violent with my mother but just loquacious and easily gave his money away to anybody who would give him a ride to Campostella when he was drunk. Caroline shared with me that our dad said he was a hardworking man. She shared with me a side of him as the dad that I never knew. How he would on Fridays bring cookies, potato chips, and chocolate candy bars home to eat. I never knew that side of my dad. I knew he loved me as his son, but he didn't know how to be a daddy to me. My three siblings, Caroline, Delores, and Michael knew him as a father, wherein I only knew him as a man I called dad.

At an early age, I remember my mother telling me I had two sisters and a brother living in Norfolk. I don't think I thought much about it because, in my heart, I already had three sisters, my cousins Jackie, Rona, and Sarah. I also felt that I had a big brother Eddie. As mentioned earlier, these were four of seven children of my mom's sister Aunt Laura and Uncle Arthur Eason. Somehow, I think I may have been in junior high school when I met my siblings for the first time. Somehow, I got to go to their home one Sunday evening. My mom was fearful that their mother, Mrs. Mary Cuffee, would do something to me because I was born the same year that my sister Caroline was born, and my mom was dating my dad, not knowing that he already had a lady, and she was pregnant the same time my

## THE THINGS I REMEMBER

mom was. Mom told me, "If she tries to feed you, don't eat the food." When I got to their home in the Berkley section of Norfolk, and I saw how nice they were and how friendly Mrs. Mary was, I felt right at home. Mrs. Mary fed, and Edward ate. I remember walking down Appomattox Street where they lived, and we went into a community store. My little sister Delores bought a cigarette which was then two for five cents. I took the cigarette and broke it up because I didn't want her to smoke. I remember us walking down the street to see our dad's brother Uncle Buster. I had a great time that day with my siblings. After that visit, Mrs. Mary and my mom started talking on the phone and became really good friends. Before Mrs. Mary died, she told me she loved me just like I was her own son. I was honored to speak at her funeral and be included in her obituary as one of her children. My dad passed away on December 29, 1980. Believe it or not, it wasn't until dad passed that I discovered that his name was Edward. I always knew him as Marvin Ashby. I was named after my dad and didn't know it.

To this day, my siblings and I love each other to "life." Delores lives in Richmond and I don't get to see her too much, but when we do, it's a whole lot of love. Michael and I talk every now and then. He's not too much into the church, but he's always telling me how he has met so many people in the church and will ask them if they know Edward Wilson or Peterman. So many folks know of me through the music and preaching ministry. Michael will call me excited, letting me know that he couldn't wait to tell them he was my brother. Caroline and I are the same age, and I talk to her more than my younger siblings. Caroline constantly attends my various concerts and programs.

I remember one year my wife Teresa and I had my siblings over for dinner with my mom. What a great day that was. The older Michael gets, the more he resembles me. On this particular day, Michael happened to be sitting at the piano when my wife called me. I was in another room, but from behind, Mike looked so much like me, she thought he was me. Boy, did we laugh at that situation! My siblings and I took a picture together, not realizing that we all had this thing for hats that resembled cowboy hats. We took a picture with our hats on. When my mother passed away, it was her request in writing that my siblings come in as her children. She need not have had to request that. My wife and I had already decided to include my siblings anyway. My mom was their mom, and their mom was my mom. I love and praise God for Caroline, Delores, and Michael, and their children, who are my nephews and nieces. I can honestly say that God placed me in a great family on my mother's side as well as my father's side of the family, and we are all closely bonded together in love. There is so much I would love to know about my father's side of the family. I praise God for allowing me to have siblings and the memory of a father that loved me and cared for me the best he could. I praise God for getting to know and love Mrs. Mary Cuffee, the mother of my siblings and her other sons, who consider me to be their brother.

On December 30, 1979, I got a call from my sister Caroline telling me that our dad had a heart attack and was taken to Norfolk General Hospital. I remember arriving at the hospital and looking through the door window towards the room where he was. I remember how the nurses and doctors seemed to be walking slowly in and out of the room. Then we received the word that our father had passed away. We were told that we could see him after they had cleaned him up. I remember walking into his room and seeing dad lying there looking like he was asleep. My dad, the man I called dad but didn't know him as such, was gone. I loved my father, and I'm proud to be the son of Sweetie and Edward Marvin Ashby. One thing he gave me were siblings who are as dear to my heart as I am to theirs.

Dad's funeral was held on Saturday, January 3, 1981, at St. Mark R.U.Z.A Church in the Berkley section of Norfolk, Virginia, where my sister Caroline is still a member. I remember picking out and taking a shirt and necktie to Fitchett Funeral Home for him. I remember Mr. Clarence Miller being at the organ playing an upbeat arrangement of "If Jesus Goes With Me, I'll Follow Anywhere." I remember the hurt of not knowing my father as a dad. Yet, I rejoiced in knowing that he was a part of my life in some small way. He was my dad. As I already stated, my siblings and I love each other to this very day. As it has been said down through the years, "The family that prays together stays together."

# 12.

# BELLS MILL THE VILLAGE

I remember when all our gang had a dream of being in the army. Well, we played army every day back in the woods behind Joe Joe's house. Yes, Joe Joe's house, the home of my mother's first cousin George Moyler (my godfather) and Alwanza (Wanza) Moyler, his wife (my mom's close friend for ninety years), was "THE PLACE." That was where all the guys met to play and have fun. It was like a recreation center for us. We spent a lot of time playing back in the woods. We often got our sticks for guns and played army. I remember my cousin Joe Joe or George Vaughan referring to himself as Lieutenant Vaughan. I don't know my character's name or what rank I held in our make-shift army, and I really didn't care. I just wanted to play army.

Back in the woods was a place where someone had dug up deep ditches for drainage and had piled the excess dirt on the side, forming hills of earth. Over the years, trees had grown on these hills, and, for some unknown reason, we gave them the name, "Pork Chop Hills." I remember taking tree branches and limbs building bridges from one hill across the ditch to another hill. I remember hiding behind trees and under bushes waiting to shoot the enemy with my stick gun making the gun noise with my mouth and lips. I remember one day Joe Joe sneaking into their house and "borrowing" a big pan. Cousin Wanza had no idea she was supporting our army soldiers. We then went into Mr. Frank Chesson's collard greens field and "borrowed "some collards. We went back into the woods after filling the pot with water from the hand pump at Cousin Wanza's house, and we lit a campfire in the woods, cooked those greens as if we were on the battlefield, and we dined. We didn't wash them off or "nothing." I spent a lot of time after that tour of army duties in the outdoor toilet. I mean, those unwashed collards worked on my stomach, and my tour of duty had to be cut short. We then discovered a new game in the woods with the trees. We would climb up the trees that were not too thick. These trees were of such a size that they would begin to lean halfway up. When you got to this point when the tree would start to lean, you had to jump and reach as high as you could and ride the tree down. The tree would slowly bend to the ground as we rode the tree down.

On one occasion, I remember Joe Joe grabbing the tree and riding it down, and halfway down, the tree snapped and broke. Down in mid-air came Joe Joe with the broken branch in his hand. Boy was that funny!

One time a rabbit died. I don't remember where it came from, but we put it in a shoebox and placed an American flag over the shoe box. I had just recently visited Jamestown on a class trip and had bought a flag. We carried the flag-draped shoebox to the woods and gave the rabbit a military funeral. We buried the rabbit in the shoebox, but you better believe I got my flag back.

Another recreation center was at the home of Mr. Colon and Mrs. Hilda Simmons. These were the parents of Ricky (Lamont) and Sweet Pea (Larry) Simmons. They also had a little sister named Pamela. Mr. Colon was one of three barbers in Bells Mill. He had a little barber's shop behind his house. Behind the barbershop was a basketball hoop made on a tree. There was an open space to play basketball, but it was surrounded by trees and tree stumps. When we would go to get a haircut, we would let Mr. Colon know we were there so that he would know what order to call us in to get what we didn't want, a haircut. Then we would run back to the basketball court and bounce around the tree stumps and shoot the ball. I can hear Mr. Colon now as he screamed through the barbershop window, "Peterman, you're next." I would go into the barbershop and get my hair cut with my sweaty head. Then, I couldn't wait to go back out and play "stump ball," I mean basketball. First, Ricky had a bicycle rim for a basketball goal. Then Mr. Colon bought him and Sweet Pea a real basketball hoop.

We also played baseball and football in their backyard. "Simmons Recreation/Barbershop" should have been the name of his establishment. It was in the barbershop that I learned a lot about being a spirit-filled being. It was not a place of gossip but a place of political talk, both local and national. Mr. Colon often talked "Sunday school talk" and "Bible study talk," and he always was concerned about our community. He was, in our eyes, the mayor of Bells Mill. Mr. Colon seemed to be the Martin Luther King Jr. of Bells Mill. He was the President Obama of the village.

We also had a place where we played baseball directly beside the residence of Mr. William (Bill) and Mrs. Minnie "Doll" Chesson. An empty field where you could find a weeping willow tree in the back of it. This is now the driveway and parking lot for The Mount Chapel in Bells Mill. There we would play baseball and climb the weeping willow tree. Directly beside the home of my Uncle Peco was our football field. This was the side yard of my kindergarten where Mrs. Hattie Todd lived. She was our kindergarten teacher and the mother of Mrs. Larue Davis, who I will talk about later. Mrs. Larue Davis was the mother of my dear lifetime friend, Andrew Davis, who would later become my bass guitar player for future concerts.

Bells Mill was more of a village than a community. Everybody was your mother and father in Bells Mill. Your response to adults was "Yes sir," "No sir," "Yes ma'am," and "No ma'am." To be in the company of adults conversing and staring at them as they conversed, was a "crime." Everybody was within their rights to whip you and send you home to await the big punishment.

The biggest dread was walking down Bells Mill Road and being slapped on the side of the head or having bottles and bricks thrown at you by white people with their hands out the window. There were certain names that stood out in Bells Mill. Names such as Mr. Will, Mr. Tom, Mrs. Ruth Massey, Mr. Colon, Cle Bell, Buster Bell, Mr. Paul, Mrs. Ruth, Sweetie, Mrs. Laura, Nubby, Sambo, Mrs. Fi Alexander, Mr. Seth McDonald, Coach Batman Barnard, PlumPie, Cherry and Pearl are so familiar. I understand that Bells Mill got its name from the sawmill owned by a white fellow named Mr. Bell. People referred to that area of Norfolk County as Bells Mill. In Bells Mill at one time were two post offices at different times, an elementary school with a full basketball court & baseball diamond, three churches, Baptist, Methodist, & Holiness, three convenience stores (Alexander's & Twines & Fosters), two dance joints, six cemeteries, and a fish market. Leaving Bells Mill and going to Great Bridge was like going to downtown Norfolk. There was no Cedar Rd. travel from Great Bridge to Deep Creek or Bakers Corner, where the closed Farm Fresh is today without going through Bells Mill. In my childhood, very few houses in Bells Mill had indoor restrooms. Almost everybody either was using an outside toilet or had used an outside toilet. Moving ahead of the book, I can remember when I first started dating my wife, I invited her over for dinner to meet my mother. Teresa needed to use the restroom, and she asked me where it was. I pointed to my mom's bedroom, where we had a bucket to do our business in. She came out and said she didn't see the restroom. I once again pointed to the bucket or pale that was used because we had no indoor bathroom. She looked at me in unbelief. To me, this was the norm, but to her, it was "what in the world?"

Bells Mill was also the home of Richmond Cedar Works (the sawmill) and a concrete company. Many men moved from North Carolina to work at these job sites, making Bells Mill their home. As a married man with children today, we have moved to different places of residence, but I always find myself with my wife constantly riding through the village known as Bells Mill. It's different now. Folk who at one time wouldn't get caught walking through the village have moved in and made it a community. New homes have been built, but there still stands, throughout the community, houses which were and forever will be the loving huts in the village called Bells Mill where all your neighbors were your mothers and fathers, and the streets were always filled with your sisters and your brothers.

I remember Mrs. Alice Roundtree's beauty salon about three houses down and across from 729 Luther Street. I would be walking out to Bells Mill Road and would hear this voice calling my name, "Peterman, come here and get me some water for my drums." She had two fifty-five gallon barrels in her salon to wash ladies' hair. Mrs. Elsie Small lived directly across the street from the salon, and she had an old hand pump at the edge of her back porch. I would get a bucket and walk back and forward, filling the bucket with water and emptying it into the fifty-five-gallon barrels until they were full. Talking about slavery, then she would give me a quarter for my labor. Once I pretended not to hear her call my name. When I got home later, I heard the voice of the almighty Sweetie calling my name, and she beat me for pretending to not hear the voice of Mrs. Alice Roundtree. It was a sin the way Sweetie whipped me. She had no mercy, no compassion, no sympathy, just a lot of energy in her body and pain from her belt.

Mrs. Elsie Small had a huge pecan tree in her yard on the side of her house. My cousin Sarah and I, along with other kids, would ride our bikes around her house and act like we fell down on the ground and we would kidnap a pocket full of pecans. They were the best pecans in the world, and we were the biggest thieves in Bells Mill. Our hearts were right because we didn't consider it is stealing; we were merely rescuing those good pecans from the dirty ground. There were so many different kinds of trees and vines to eat from in Bells Mill. There was a grapevine behind my Aunt Laura's house. My Uncle Nick owned a grapevine on Luther Street in a field between Mr. Charlie Walker's house and Mr. Hurley Satterfield's house. Pear trees were found in the field across from our home at 729, owned by Mr. Joe Jake (Joseph Riddick) and Mrs. Ida Riddick. Also, there was one on my Uncle Peco's property. My godfather and cousin George Moyler and Alwanza Moyler had a fig tree in their front yard. There were cherry trees and apple trees all over Bells Mill.

I remember the pear tree just across the ditch from our front porch at 729 Luther Street. Mr. Joe Jake used to say to us, "Y'all chillens' can get the pears off the ground but don't mess with the ones on the tree." So, we would get sticks and two by fours, and we would throw them up into the tree and knock the pears down to the ground so that we could legally get them in obedience to his request.

I remember my grandmother Mama Creasy taking me to the strawberry field, located on Kempsville Road just down the street from Little Zion Baptist Church. The area is now filled with beautiful homes. If you've been to the 7-11 stores on the corner of Kempsville Road and Green Tree Road near the Huddle House Restaurant, this was the location of the old strawberry field. Many acres of land where the 7-11 and the Greenbrier Christian Academy is located now is where the strawberry field was. I remember the big two-story house that stood in the midst of the field like an old mansion on a slave plantation. We would ride there on an old school bus and were given ten-quart basket containers on a big wooden tray with wire handles. We would go into the field and pick strawberries filling up the little quart baskets. Mama Creasy would tell me, "Edward, don't pick the strawberries that have some green on them, they are not ripe yet." So, I would pick and eat, pick, and eat, pick, and eat. When the little quart baskets were full, we would take them to the big house and turn them in. They would be inspected, and we were given ten cents for each basket. Did you hear me? I said ten cents, one dime, two nickels, ten pennies. All that work for ten cents. If I was paid for all the strawberries I ate while picking in the field, I probably could buy the whole field. We wore old clothes and a straw hat, and we looked like slaves out in the field, but I must say it was a lot of fun considering I could eat while I worked.

When I read about the prodigal son in the Bible, I'm reminded of his experience feeding the swine and desiring to eat the husk that they ate because he was so hungry. Well, I've never had that desire, but I did have to feed the hogs. As I recall, several men in Bells Mill owned hog pens; Mr. Bishop Bell, Mr. Edward McDonald, Mr. Seth McDonald, Mr. Henry Hargrove, Mr. Vernon Bell Sr., Mr. Henry Ricks, and then there was Mr. George Moyler, who was my godfather as well as my mother's first cousin. It was his hogs that I would mix up the slop in a fifty-five-gallon barrel with all the old bread, vegetables, sour milk, water, and whatever else could be put in it. It smelt terrible, but I would mix the slop with a large stick, then take a bucket and scoop it out, pouring it into the hog trough for the pigs and hogs to eat. I promise you when you've been around pigs or hogs for a few minutes, when you leave, you will smell like them. I remember seeing my godfather, Uncle George, hang a hog up on a tree branch by his feet. Then I remember him taking a knife and splitting the hog straight down the belly. I remember seeing all of the insides come out into a large tin pale or bucket. Then the guts were cleaned (still stinking), and the various parts of the hog were turned into a delicacy meal. This consisted of pig feet, pig tales, pig ears, and one of my wife's favorites that I "DO NOT" like, hog chitlings' (Bill Cosby once said he thinks they misspelled the word).

# THE THINGS I REMEMBER

In the village, it was sometimes dangerous to walk up and down the street of Bells Mill Road. We always had trouble with the white folk Ku Klux Klan (KKK) coming through our community. They would drive through, put their hands out of their car windows, and hit you side the head as they sped by. I remember once a car came by, and some white boys hit my cousin Eddie Eason, the son of my Aunt Laura, side the head. His car was in front of Mr. Will's store being used by his father, Uncle Arthur. The car was pointed in the same direction that the car was going with the white boys in it. My understanding is that he jumped in his car and caught the white boys. My Uncle Peco just happened to be driving by when Eddie approached the white boy's car. Uncle Peco always carried a baseball bat in his car in case there was trouble with our blue-eyed brothers. He took the bat out and made the white boys wait in line to be whipped by Cousin Eddie.

I remember once when I had come in from a choir rehearsal, just as I got out of the car, a group of white boys drove by and stormed the front concrete porch of Mr. Twine's store located right in front of my house with bottles and bricks while screaming "NIGGERS, NIGGERS." I remember a yellow jeep that came through our community on some Friday nights with white boys throwing items at whoever they saw. One Friday night, the fellows were standing around chilling and waiting. There is only one way in and out of Bells Mill, so when the jeep came by throwing things and screaming horrible things, the fellows were waiting and ready. The boys from Bells Mill threw bricks, sticks, and pieces of concrete and baptized the yellow jeep with revenge. To my recollection, the jeep never came through Bells Mill again. It's hard to believe that Bells Mill is now a diverse community with blacks and whites living throughout the community. Back in the day, you couldn't pay a white person to walk through Bells Mill. Now they're walking, running, riding bicycles, walking dogs, and taking ownership of the village known as "Bells Mill." Dr. Martin Luther King Jr. would be proud of where Bells Mill has come from. Then, Bells Mill was a village, but now it is a community. Wow!

Bells Mill was the product of some professional people. Mr. Charles Stukes became an NFL football player for the Baltimore Colts as a defensive back, winning the Super Bowl one year. He later played with the Los Angeles Rams. The entire Stukes family was active in sports of all kinds. Bells Mill also produced two judges, Judge Luther Edmonds, Chief Judge of the Norfolk City Court system, and Judge Howard E. Bell, who presided over the famous Central Park murder in New York City. We also had a university professor Dr. E. Curtis Alexander, who was instrumental in some of the history told in this book. He is a historian author with studies about Colored troops in the Civil War, which his grandfather March Corprew was a part of. My cousin, Wilson Williams of Bells Mill, was an R&B recording artist.

As I reflect on my childhood days, I can recall all the relatives I had in my family who were no blood relation to me. I've mentioned my Uncle Randolph and Aunt May Little, who were like my second mom and dad. Uncle Randolph had two brothers, and because they were his brothers, I called them uncle also. I would go to Uncle Randolph Little's house on Saturdays at 344 Waters Road, Chesapeake, Virginia, to cut his grass with his lawnmower. This area was known as Dawson Town because so many in the Dawson family lived in that area. Uncle Randolph's yard seemed to me as a young boy to be so big. It took me just about all day to cut it. He would pick me up and take me to his house in his Galaxy 500, which had wings on the back like the old Batman, Batmobile. It also had push buttons for the gear change. His wife, Aunt May, would get me to go to their chicken house and get some fresh eggs, and then she would send me to one of their five apple trees to get some apples. Aunt May would fix breakfast with the fresh eggs and fried apples from the apples I had picked from their tree. Then, I would proceed to cut the grass, which I thought I would never finish. Sometimes Uncle Randolph would ask me to wash his car, which I did. It looked better to me before I washed it than after I washed it. I remember begging Uncle Randolph to let me move the car up a little bit. He would say to me, "Naw son, taint twile." Those words meant, "There was no need to" and they stick with me today. In their home, they had an extra bedroom that Aunt May told me belonged to me even though I never spent a night there as I can remember. This was a couple that I loved as if they were my own parents. Aunt May was my Sunday school teacher, and Uncle Randolph was my favorite deacon at the church. Now, I will tell you about Uncle Randolph's two brothers.

Uncle Henry Little, who was married to my mother's first cousin, Irene Roberts Little, was Uncle Randolph's brother. He lived about four or five houses down from Uncle Randolph on Waters Road. Uncle Henry, or as I affectionately called him, Uncle Chick was a member of Mt. Lebanon Baptist Church, where I was a member, and he and his wife Cousin Irene sang in the senior choir. One of the main songs he led as he was slow-talking and slow-moving was "Give Me A Heart Like Thine." I can see him now reaching up to touch his eyeglasses as he sang, "Give me a heart that knows no ill, give me the grace to do thy will, pardon and cleanse this old heart of mind Lord give me a heart like thine." As a young man coming up when there were times, I needed some financial assistance, Uncle Chick was always willing to help me and give me words of encouragement. He had a Ford LTD with the same body style as my 1975 Ford LTD. This was my second car, and I remember I needed to get it inspected, but I knew the tires were worn, and I really didn't have the money to get them, so he let me come to his house and take "all" four of his tires off his car and put my worn tires on his car. I put his good tires on my car and got it inspected. Then, I came right back to his house and traded the tires back the way they were. I was young, and I had the energy to do what had to be done. My car passed inspection because he cared about me. Not long after, I had sense enough to apply for a Firestone credit card and got it. I bought myself four brand new 721 Goodyear tires.

Uncle Chick also had a beautiful garden beside his house, and he would call my mom and tell her, "Tell Peterman to come on by here and get some collard greens." Uncle Chick was such a wonderful man who didn't put his nose in everybody's business. I loved him, and I'm grateful to call him my uncle (even though he wasn't).

Uncle Randolph also had a brother named Anderson Little, whose house still stands today and his store. When you first turn on Waters Road, there is a gray house on the left side of the road. This was the home of Mr. Anderson Little and his wife, Mrs. Hurly Bly Little. I called them Uncle Anderson and Aunt Hurly. I wasn't as close to Uncle Anderson, but I remember him owning the community convenience store that still stands and operates today, although under different management. The store is on Waters Road at the intersection of Washington Drive. I remember on Saturdays when I went to Uncle Randolph's home to cut his grass, I would walk three houses down to Uncle Anderson's home. I met one of my best friends today Wayne Mann who lived next door to Uncle Anderson. When you turn on to Waters Road off Cedar Road, you actually are driving right through where Wayne's house used to be. I do remember going down to Uncle Anderson's store and, of course, being a "greedy butt," I ate whatever he would let me have. One day Uncle Anderson went into his little office in the back of the store. I don't know if he was sick or not, but I do know that it was there in the store one day that he took "flight" to Glory. Uncle Anderson passed away in that little room in his store. These were the Little brothers who were big men in my life. Randolph, Henry, and Anderson Little, the men who played a father's role in my life.

# THE THINGS I REMEMBER

1955 - Alberta Sweetie Wilson pregnant with me

My father - Edward Marvin Ashby

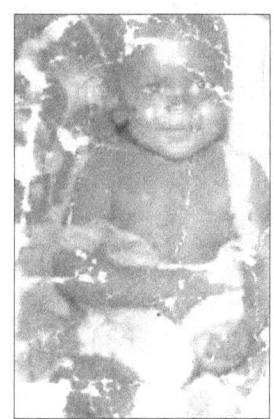

Me

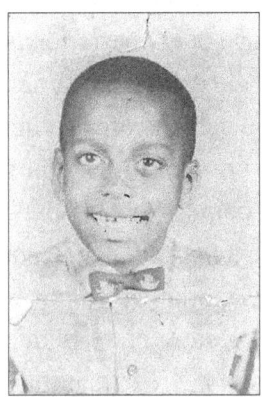

My first grade photo

Me at the Washington D.C. City Zoo

Me standing on Luther St. holding Angela Griffin with Calvin Griffin beside me

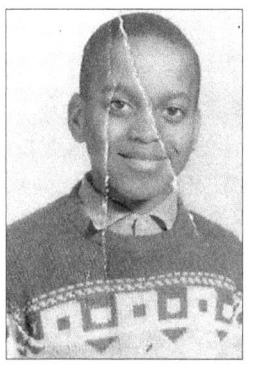
Me at Bells Mill Elementary School in the 5th grade

My 1st car parked at 937 Bells Mill Rd.

My piano donated by Lees Chapel AME Church

Me and my mother

Me in the Eastern Star Youth Department to my left Mrs. Goldie Walker

Me in Mt. Lebanon Baptist Church Sunday School Choir – back row. Cousin Verona Eason 2nd girl on 2nd row to my right. Her sister, now my pastor Dr. Sarah E Williams, 1st girl on front row to the right.

## THE THINGS I REMEMBER

Me in Air Force ROTC
Crestwood High School

Left- Me in Air Force ROTC
Great Bridge High School

My 1973 graduation photo
Great Bridge High School

1974 attending Norfolk
State College

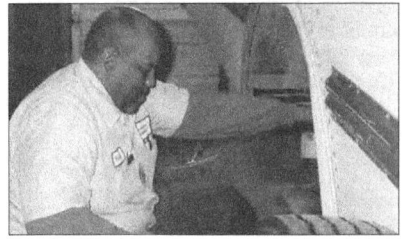

Tire Technician Chesapeake Schools
Transportation Dept.

Tire Technician Chesapeake Schools
Transportation Dept.

November 25, 1978 marrying the love of my life

Early family portrait -standing Sherita, Teresa -seated Keisha, me -babies Nikki, Ashley

Me and my wife Teresa at a marriage retreat

Me and my wife Teresa

Our 4 daughters -Ashley, Nikki, Sherita, Keisha

# THE THINGS I REMEMBER

I'm with my mentor Dr. Richard Smallwood

I'm with my siblings -Caroline, Delores, and Michael Amos

Me with my mother Alberta "Sweetie" Wilson

# 13.

# WE'RE MOVING ON UP

We moved from 729 Luther Street, down the street, to a white one-story house later painted forest green by my Uncle Nick & my stepbrother Benjamin Wilson. The house was located at 937 Bells Mill Rd. Just to the side of our new home was another house painted grey about 12 feet away. Our house was back off the main road and in front of it was an old store. Uncle Nick's biological father, Mr. Edward Bell, owned these two houses and the store. Once Mr. Bell passed away, all three buildings belonged to Uncle Nick. When we moved in, I thought we were moving into a house in the Georgetown community of Las Gaviotas (considered to be two upscale communities). We now had running water, meaning turning the faucet on and letting the water run, and I no longer had to use a hand pump. However, we didn't have hot water. Instead of chopping wood and bringing in the coal for heat, we had an oil heater and propane gas kitchen stove. We still did not have indoor plumbing, but there was a brand new outdoor toilet in the backyard. I thank God for all we did have.

Our new home had a screened-in front porch. When you walked into the house, you were in the living room. Just to the left was my mom's bedroom. Then you walked into the dining room. Just to the left of it was my bedroom. Then you walked into the kitchen.

Just to the left of it was the back porch. This is where I lived until I married and got my own place.

I thought I was in a brand-new house. I had my own bedroom. I didn't have to cut and bring in wood and coal. I remember many days sitting on the front porch enjoying the fresh air when suddenly, this smell came out of nowhere. There was a store directly in front of our house. To the right side of the store was a house occupied by Mr. Wiley and Mrs. Olivia Crandell. Our driveway ran between the store and the Crandell's house. Behind their home and about fifteen yards to the side of our front porch was their outdoor toilet. Needless to say, when the air hit it right, it was time to go in the house.

My mom was a very neat and clean person who raised her son to be a good house cleaner. Our furniture was old but nice. In the living room was a green sofa, a wing chair, and my old upright piano, which I mentioned earlier, was given to me by my mom's church, Lees Chapel AME Church. My mom's bedroom was nice and neat. She had a wooden box with a toilet seat on it, this was her master bathroom. The next room was the dining room. Here we had a shiny table with orange-covered plastic chairs. A small black and white television, a recliner, and an oil heater. I was so grateful for that oil heater because it meant I did not have to chop wood anymore. My bedroom was nice and congested, with junk I refused to throw away. I had an electric fan in my window in the summertime with the cool night air blowing in. Needless to say, I woke up many mornings with the sniffles and my bed wet from the damp dew blowing from the outside into my room. However, it felt like an air conditioner that we couldn't afford.

Our kitchen was small but cozy. We had a gas stove which was operated by gas propane tanks outside. Instead of the electric breaker boxes that we have today, there was an electric panel box somewhere in our house that housed fuses that had to be screwed in. When a fuse blew out, you had to unscrew the bad fuse and screw in a new fuse. Many nights I would be in my bedroom trying to be an electrician, fixing wires, electrical cords, extension cords, even radios, and record players. I'd put two wires together that shouldn't be put together. Suddenly, all the lights would go out, and my mom would say, "Edvard, what are you doing in there?" Of course, my response would always be, "I ain't doin' nothing much." I'm surprised the house didn't catch fire. At this time in my life, I not only had a new home, but I also attended a new school a year later.

In the 7th grade at Crestwood Junior High School, we still lived at 729 Luther Street, but in the 8th grade, we moved to 937 Bells Mill Road. So, from the 7th or 8th grade until I became a married man, I resided at 937 Bells Mill Road. Memories; gone but not forgotten. I remember the Saturdays cutting the grass and the daily pleasures of taking the indoor toilet to empty in the outdoor toilet. I remember the little pump house on the side of the back porch that caused us to have running water. I remember putting a light bulb in the pump house to keep the pipes from freezing during the winter. We didn't have hot water, but we did have running water. We didn't have an air conditioner, but we had floor fans, we didn't have central heat, but we had an oil heater.

As I look back on my life and see whence, I've come, I can say that God has truly been good to me. He brought me, kept me, and promised even in this retirement season to never leave me or forsake me. God is just that good.

# 14.

# OVER MY HEAD, I HEAR MUSIC

At some point, I believe it was in the sixth grade, I developed a heart for the piano. When I was young, I would go to my Aunt Laura's house, and next door to her lived Morris and Carol Etheridge. They had two daughters, and one of them had a little play organ about as big as a shoebox. You would use the buttons to the left and get harmony sounds while playing the keys' melody. I would go over to their house quite often to play that little organ. I had a passion for playing the piano. I remember one day Carol told me that the organ was broken. Interpretation, I'm sick of you coming over here with all that noise. I must confess, I understand. I was there "every day." I was worrisome. One day during the summer, I went to work with my mom at the home of a white lady named Mrs. Ridge. Down in her basement, she had a set of drums, a guitar, and a piano for her sons. I remember messing with the drums and plucking on the guitar. But what really got my attention was the piano. It never left me.

Being raised in Bells Mill, we had a Methodist church, a Holiness church, and a Baptist church. My grandmother, Mrs. Creasy Williams, was a devoted member of Lees Chapel AME Church. My mother Sweetie, and her brother Uncle Willis (Peco), followed her in membership. My grandfather was an inactive (didn't go to church) member of Mt. Lebanon Baptist Church. My Aunt Laura Eason and my Aunt Sarah Nichols (Sugardoll) followed him or, should I say, represented his absence. Uncle Lloyd kind of followed no one. He was a great, wonderful, nice, good-looking man with pretty wavy hair. He decided his church would be where worldly communion was observed by those who preferred not to attend church. Uncle Peco's children, of course, followed their dad and our grandmother to Lee's Chapel. Aunt Laura's kids followed her to Mt. Lebanon Baptist Church, so I followed her because I was close to Jackie, Rona, and Sarah.

I developed a great love for my church. I would sit in the "Amen" corner with Uncle Randolph Little. During those days, Lee's Chapel AME had services on the first and third Sundays, and Mt. Lebanon Baptist had services on the second and fourth Sundays. I became a member of the junior ushers' board and the Sunday school choir directed by Mrs. Goldie Walker and accompanied by the music of Mrs. Alberta McDonald. Man, I can still hear the song "I Promised the Lord That I Would Hold Out." Mrs. Goldie directed us with those short arms as she would get happy and scream, "YEA, SING CHILDREN."

I remember when I first started playing the piano about the age of twelve or thirteen. Whenever I played the piano in the sanctuary, folks, including my Uncle Randolph Little, told me not to play that piano because I would get it out of tune. There was an "old" upright piano in the back of the church that I was free to play. When we had Vacation Bible School, I couldn't wait for the afternoon break to come. Vacation Bible School was held in the morning and then we would break for lunch. We would walk to the store owned by Mr. William Alexander (Mr. Will) and then return to the church for the evening program. Vacation Bible School was always held in the back of the church at Mt. Lebanon in a large meeting room where the upright piano was located. After the lunch break, I would get to the old upright piano and play the songs we sang. Mrs. Goldie would get so excited that she would sometimes get happy in the spirit! I didn't understand her reaction until I became a man and understood what it meant to "be filled" with the spirit of God. I thought she was getting happy because we sounded good! Now I understand that she was happy because she knew and appreciated God's goodness, mercy, and power.

I remember Friday nights during the week of Vacation Bible School, we would have our Vacation Bible School closing. I provided the music throughout the week, and we had a great time singing, clapping, and having church. Then on that Friday night, the Sunday school pianist, Mrs. Alberta McDonald, would say to me, "I'm playing tonight, son." She was one of the church's seniors who only played by sheet music, and the other kids were quite disappointed. Needless to say, I was really hurt as a young child. We could not sing the uplifting songs we had sung during the day. Instead, we had to sing the cute Sunday school songs that she played by music. The few songs they did sing that she couldn't play were sung with no music because I wasn't allowed to play the "good" piano in the sanctuary.

I remember one Sunday during Sunday school, Mr. Will Alexander, the chairman of the deacons' board and the owner of our local grocery store, was sitting in the Amen corner as he always did. I understand he asked a question in Sunday school, but he slumped over and passed away before the answer could come. That next day (Monday) was our first day of Vacation Bible School. The door was directly next to the sanctuary where Mr. Will had passed away, which led to the classroom I was in for Bible school. Instead of discussing our lesson, we talked about how Mr. Will had died the day before. My dear sweet cousin, Sarah, who says she didn't mean to do it, walked through the dark sanctuary to get to our classroom. She then very slowly opened the door, which made a squeaking noise. Linda Bell, in a loud voice, declared, "It's Mr. Will!" Needless to say, all ran from the room with loud screams of terror. Mrs. Goldie Walker, our Vacation Bible School director and who was supposed to be there to protect us, got up and ran out of the room. Mrs. Goldie and Pat Johnson tried to get out of the room simultaneously, and they both were stuck in the doorway. Couldn't tell you who crossed over the finish line first, but that event I will never forget. Mrs. Goldie Walker was the Martin Luther King Jr. of the Bells Mill community. She organized and was the president for years of the NAACP Chesapeake Branch. But, unlike Dr. King, she was indeed a background person who was totally committed to the caring of our Black community. Her husband, Mr. Charlie Walker, was the person to call when there was a funeral in the community. I can see him now with those sharp-pointed shoes, with a piece of paper in his hand, writing the names of those who had volunteered to drive their cars in the funeral procession, lifting families' burden.

When I got older, I left the junior ushers board and joined the #2 Choir under the leadership of my first mentor Mrs. Rosa Cuffee Worlds. Rosa was the organist for the #2 Choir. I used to love to hear and watch Rosa play with her own unique style. I gained a great interest in playing the piano and the organ watching her play. I would go down to the home of my friend Andrew Davis who became a renowned bass guitar player in the Tidewater area. Andrew thought I was at his home to play with him, but for real, his mom Mrs. Larue Davis, a great organist of those days, owned a Baldwin organ in her house that I loved to play. I credit Mrs. Larue for encouraging me to play in other keys. She never told me she didn't feel like hearing the organ played. She always allowed me to play it, even when her husband, Mr. Charles Davis, brought her a brand-new beautiful Baldwin organ. As I played, Mrs. Larue would sing, and Andrew would be outside waiting for me to come out and play.

Joining the #2 Choir at the old Mt. Lebanon Baptist Church played a significant role in my musical history. It was there that I tried to lead my first solo. I remember Rosa told me to sing, "I'll

## OVER MY HEAD, I HEAR MUSIC

Be Caught up to Meet Him in the Air." I remember one second Sunday when Rosa "hit up on" the song. She played it in the wrong key, and I came out sounding like Tarzan in the jungles of Africa calling for his elephants.

My beginning in music, I believe, began in my mother's womb. I had the ear to harmonize notes when I sang. Never had a great voice, but I knew my parts. When my cousin Mr. Sampson (Sambo) Moyler saw my potential to play because I was playing by ear, he decided to give me music lessons for free. I would walk down to his house in Bells Mill on Alexander Lane with my beginner's book and practice until he came home from work. Then, of course, I would stop practicing and begin to play by ear when I would hear the voice of his wife, Cousin Mammie Moyler, calling from the kitchen as she prepared his dinner. She would yell, "Peterman, you've better practice your music book before Sambo gets home." This went on for a short time. Once I kept hitting a wrong note and Cousin Sambo "popped" me beside my head. Well, that took care of the free lessons. Never went back to him again.

It was then that my non-DNA Uncle Randolph volunteered to pay for me to take lessons under a man named Mr. Creekmore, who was also giving lessons to my cousins Beverly and Ovid. This man was so nice, but he was old, and he kept going to sleep as I played. I'd be playing and watching him go to sleep. I'd stop playing and continue to watch him until he woke up. Then I would go to the last measure of the music lesson for the day. What a waste of Uncle Randolph's money. Needless to say, that didn't go over too well.

I found myself simply using what God had given me, which was the gift to play by ear. I would pick up songs that I heard Mrs. Rosa Worlds play on Sundays and play them. When I was about fifteen years old, I began to play along with Rosa on second Sundays when the #2 choir would sing. I, along with a few other members of the #2 choir, began to participate in a music workshop with a very talented fellow named Dwight Steele. I would watch Dwight as he conducted his workshop choir rehearsals. I heard how he taught parts to the sopranos, altos, and tenors. I loved to listen to him playing the piano, and when he got on the Hammond organ, there was nothing to say but "WOW!" I learned so much from Dwight, and God was setting me up for a blessing through him.

I remember how I began to imitate Rosa on the piano. I started to play songs she played mocking or imitating her. I had no idea I was developing my ear for the sounds of the future. I was just having fun. Finally, Rosa began allowing me to play the sermonic songs with her playing the organ and me playing the piano. I remember how nervous I was. The organ was in the choir stand, but the piano was on the floor. I would go down shaking and praying I didn't mess up. Then one day, Rosa decided she wanted to lead a song and let me play it on the organ. The song was "Show Some Sign." I got to the organ, looked down at my feet on the pedals and the two roles of keys on the organ, and almost passed out. It seemed that song went on forever. Then Rosa had the nerve to get happy. I didn't know what to do, so I just got up. I had done my job and was glad it was over.

Through Rosa Worlds, I got numerous opportunities to play with her, and I learned so much from her. Even today, I've said so many times, "When you hear me playing, you hear Rosa playing." I will never forget those who were a blessing in my life to get me to where I am today with my little gift of music.

The #2 Choir would go out from Sunday to Sunday, from church to church for programs and choir anniversaries. One Sunday, we went to Zion Bethel United Church of Christ in Portsmouth for the Zionett Gospel Singers anniversary. I was about sixteen or seventeen years old. I think I was a junior in high school. As I often did, I played with Rosa for the #2 choir of our church. Sometime during or after the program, a young lady named Beverly Mason came up to me and said that she was the organist for the junior choir of New Oak Grove Baptist Church located in a place called Blackwater.

I had never heard of the place until Mrs. Mable Townsend, the sister of Morris Etheridge Jr., asked me to play for kindergarten graduation there about a year earlier. Those young folk sounded good in that junior choir. She said she was leaving to teach school in Boston and asked me to play for them until she returned. So, from my junior year in high school until I was married with four children, I played for that choir. I remained at the church playing for the junior choir, which later became the young adult choir, for nearly thirty years.

I've played for many, many choirs over the years, but the chemistry between that choir and I was and remains so powerful. Back in 2011, I was blessed to go back to New Oak Grove and conduct a reunion concert. Choir members from the time I began to play there until the time I left came back. Some came from out of town. Some have now joined other churches, but we came together. The first night of rehearsal was so emotional. Every time someone came through the door for rehearsal, cheers went up, and tears came down. The first song I went over was one of the first songs I played for them some thirty years earlier, entitled "Lord Keep Me Day by Day. The only thing missing was the silenced voice of one of my most devoted and gifted choir members, Bro. Ronnie Holmes, who had passed away years earlier. At that concert, we were blessed to have a full house even though it rained. The unique thing was even at the end of the concert of about sixteen songs, the church was still full. I believe we all had Ronnie on our minds that night.

Ronnie Holmes was a very gifted man of God. One who was not ashamed to let you know that he lived a homosexual lifestyle until God turned his life around in his earlier years. I remember some funny things about Ronnie, who, as a youth, was loud, a comedian, and as a young boy, he didn't get along with a girl in the choir by the name of Bessie Boone. They were like oil and water. They just could not get along. They were like a positive pole and a negative pole on a battery. Yet, deep down inside, they did like each other, they just couldn't get along. Ronnie as a young boy was an organist's nightmare in choir rehearsal. Always had something smart to say and wouldn't shut up. I was young and immature myself. Once I got tired of hearing his mouth, and I stood up on the organ pedals and sailed at him a National Baptist Hymnal. I missed, but it got him quiet for a little while.

One time the young folk in the choir who were from twelve to eighteen got on my nerve so bad until I vowed not to be at church to play for them that following Sunday. They didn't believe me. I wasn't driving at the time, so I would catch a ride with an elderly man and his wife, Deacon Hardy and Mrs. Viola Williams. I called Deacon Williams that Saturday night and simply told them that I didn't need a ride the next day. It broke my heart to do it, but I didn't show up for morning service because the young folk had plucked my last nerve. That Sunday evening, I got an unexpected visit from three Deacons of the church informing me that they understood and that I had done the right thing, and anytime it happens again, please let them know. Ronnie's grandfather, Mr. Charlie Holmes, told me "Please call me if that boy acts stupid again. I'm gonna get him when I get home." Then, they gave me my paycheck of $75.00 and left. Things got a lot better after that.

I think it was in 1993 or 1994 that Ronnie Holmes got sick. Ronnie had joined my group, The Edward J. Wilson Ensemble, and had given his life back "totally" to Christ. Ronnie became ill with acquired immunodeficiency syndrome (AIDS). The Ensemble supported him and showed love to him and for him. We, as well as Ronnie, followed all precautions. Ronnie was such a devoted friend and singer who really loved God and had a great gift of singing. He was always there when I needed him. He was a faithful servant of the Most High God. We hugged Ronnie and let him know that we were there for him. Ronnie eventually got worst and was put into the hospital at Leigh Memorial. I went to see him about a week before he passed away. As I entered the room with a mask and gloves on, I looked at my friend lying there in his bed of affliction, or should I say his bed of transformation. Ronnie was sleeping, and as I looked at him, I saw how thin he was. His teeth seemed to be too large for his mouth because his face had become so small. There was shed skin on the bed, and when he woke up. I said to him, "Hey Ronnie, how are you?"

This young man, this converted Christian, this born-again believer who knew he was dying said to me, "Edward, I'm hurting but Oh, Praise the Lord, thank you, Jesus, my soul is happy." Talking about being encouraged, I dared not to complain about anything. What an example to show faithfulness in the Almighty God. Ronnie died in 1994 and had a homegoing service that was like no other. The young adult choir of New Oak Grove sang every song Ronnie had ever sung without a leader. All of us in our spirits could hear Ronnie's voice leading each song.

About a year later, in June 1995, I got a surprise visit from Ronnie's mom and sister. They came to my home to give me a Father's Day gift that hangs in my office at home and a copy in my office at the church. A year after Ronnie was buried, his mom found the courage to go into Ronnie's bedroom and closet and clean it out. In his closet, inside a shoebox, were some papers from Ronnie's class he was taking at Tidewater Community College. Ronnie had written an essay entitled "The Most Interesting Person I Know." It starts out, "The most interesting person I know would have to be Edward Wilson, the director of the Young Adult Choir. He instills in his choir members a sense of moral obligation and a deep-felt desire to sing God's praises through song." Then he described me and talked about my love for my family and my commitment to my church choirs. Finally, he ended the paper by saying, "Edward Wilson is truly a remarkable person."

This paper means so much to me, and I will forever be humbly grateful to his mother and family for this beautifully designed stationery with a soft background picture of a baby grand piano. I placed the paper in the picture frame with a photo of Ronnie that he had given to my wife and me some years earlier. May God rest his soul.

Some members of the Young Adult Choir got married and had children who later joined the same choir with their parents. It was an honor to rejoin them at a Young Adult Choir Reunion Concert in 2011. I had served as the organist for New Oak Grove Baptist Church for twenty-seven years. It was such a joyous experience to return to New Oak Grove after being gone for nearly fifteen years to conduct a reunion concert. Choir members who were no longer members of the church and those who were still there came together in unity to praise God in songs. We had set up about five rehearsals for the concert. On that first Monday night, as my wife and I walked into the sanctuary where the choir members were waiting, some we had not seen in years, thunderous applause went up as tears were shed with hugs and greetings of joy. The same happened each time a choir member entered the sanctuary.

I've played for many choirs and groups over the years, but there was and is a special bond between my former Young Adult Choir of New Oak Grove Baptist Church in the Blackwater section of Virginia Beach and me.

The following year after the reunion concert, Joann Foreman Mason, one of the former choir members, passed away. Her brother Alfred Foreman Jr. was my best friend and president of the young adult choir, what seems like forever. I attended Joann's funeral, and by request, we called up all the former young adult choir members. They came up and blessed the overflow crowd singing one of our old songs, which I believed was the testimony of Joann and her husband, Cecil. That song was "Give Yourself to Jesus." The words are a testimony of my life to all who hear me play and direct choirs all over the Tidewater area. We all must give ourselves to Jesus because we don't have much time. So, just put all your trust in Him. God will take of you.

I really think the most touching time of my music ministry was when my wife, with the assistance of the Edward J. Wilson Ensemble, a gospel group I organized and am the director and musician of, gave me an appreciation/show your love service in November 2013. The service was held at the New Light Church, where the pastor is my friend and brother, Bishop Darryl McClary, Sr. Many former choir members, family, and friends gathered to honor my fifty years of service in the music ministry. My grandchildren escorted me into the church as I was honored with a standing ovation. Various musicians and singers gave encouraging words of how I had affected them positively in ministry, both preaching and music. It made me feel good that God had touched so many by using me as a humble servant.

I received a special letter and photo from President Barack Obama and the White House congratulating me for my years of service. I also got a letter of congratulations from the mayor of our city, Mayor Alan P. Krasnoff. Also, to my surprise, a video was sent by my music mentor Dr. Richard Smallwood, the famous gospel artist in the world of gospel music. Richard Smallwood actually called my name out and gave words of inspiration. I had been blessed some years before to participate in a gospel music workshop with Richard Smallwood sponsored by the First Baptist Church of South Hill, where my friend, Rev. Michael Toliver, is the pastor. There I got to shake hands and talk to Mr. Smallwood, and I was able to get his autograph. Following the showing of his video sent from Washington D. C., the combined former choir members under the direction of Bishop Darryl sang Richard Smallwood's song "Total Praise."

Oh my God! What a wonderful time of celebration! My wife gave me the sweetest words of encouragement. I thank God that she has always supported me as I have played for various churches throughout the years. As soon as I became lazy or didn't want to do anything, she pushed me to do it. She, together with my children, elevates me as a musician to a whole new level. It is a gift to be married to someone who really cares about you and supports you in all your endeavors. God has blessed me in so many ways in my music ministry. I am so grateful to God for the gift of ear and playing the organ, piano, and keyboard. I praise God for those who have paved the way and set the example of true music ministry. To God be the glory for the things He has done.

I've served as organist or minister of music for many churches over the past fifty-plus years. New Oak Grove Baptist, Virginia Beach, Lee's Chapel AME, Chesapeake, Little Zion Baptist, Chesapeake, St. James AME, Norfolk, Mt. Olive COGIC, Chesapeake, Mt. Lebanon Baptist, Chesapeake, New Mt. Olive AME, Chesapeake, First Baptist Church Crestwood, Chesapeake, Bethel Baptist, Norfolk, Trinity Baptist Faith Diamond, Chesapeake, Union Bethel Baptist, Chesapeake, Centerville AME, Chesapeake, and presently, The Church of the Living God Center for Change Chesapeake. I've also been blessed to serve as a musician for several gospel groups such as The Edward Wilson Singers of Bells Mill, The Gospellets of Virginia Beach, The Voices of Faith of Chesapeake, and The Angelics of Chesapeake, and others that I can't think of. I praise God for allowing me to work with some of the most loving believers. Of course, some were always busy trying to come against what God had led me to do in music ministry, but these folk never stopped me from giving one hundred percent of my dedication to whatever ministry I was supporting. I love God, and I love what He has given me the ability to do. Not that I think that I'm all that in music ministry, but such as I have, I give my all with my choirs.

God has blessed me in so many ways in music ministry. The ear to pick up and play whatever I hear, a supporting wife who has always been by my side and makes me feel like I am the greatest musician in the world, and daughters who love and support my music ministry by singing with and for whatever choirs I need them to sing with and for. Many nights I felt I was tired and didn't feel like doing what needed to be done or when I was having a hard time learning the new arrangement of songs of today, and that beautiful angel named Teresa (my wife) would always encourage me and remind me that I can do all things through Christ who strengthens me. When I began to write original songs, I would write them and teach them to my daughters for soundcheck and get input from my wife. I've been blessed to play hymns, black gospels from James Cleveland's era, and the most current gospel music. As mentioned before, Rev. Richard Smallwood has played a significant role in my musical career. During a workshop at First Baptist South Hill, Rev. Smallwood taught us songs for the workshop concert and gave us valuable information concerning the music ministry. In the workshop, he asked if there were any questions. I raised my hand and asked if there was a chance that he would play an instrumental on the piano at the concert. He paused and looked up and said with a smile, "We'll see." At the concert, he played an instrumental that had me in tears. A few months later, he put out a CD at the Jericho City of Praise, and for the first time, he played an instrumental medley, "It Is Well With My Soul and Come Ye Disconsolate." I often wonder if my suggestion placed it in his spirit to do an instrumental. I had never known him to do that before.

After the concert held at Oscar Smith High School in Chesapeake, Virginia, my wife and our daughters got into our car to leave. As we drove behind the school to turn around, we saw Rev. Smallwood exiting the building to get in the car to take him, I believe to the airport or to his hotel. My wife being who she is, put the window down and screamed, "RIIICHHHARD." He looked over and waved and laughed as he was getting into the car.

I have the greeting that Mr. Smallwood videoed for my appreciation/show your love celebration downloaded on my computer today. I thank God for the gift he has given Rev. Richard Smallwood, as well as for his music. At every opportunity, I study and teach his music. Today, he is my mentor in the world of gospel music.

I've had other local mentors, including Mrs. Rosa Worlds and Mr. Clarence Barnard, my gym teacher in junior high school. Also, Mr. Barnard's cousin, Mrs. Alberta Curtis Minters, was a mentor. She was the musician for the recording gospel group known as the Gospel Union Singers. Both Mr. Barnard and Mrs. Minters are from the village called Bells Mill. I'm a blessed man to have these people in my life as mentors of music.

# 15.

# BLACK & WHITE TOGETHER

From first to sixth grade, I attended Bells Mill Elementary School. From seventh to eighth grades, I attended Crestwood Junior High, and from ninth to tenth grades, I attended Crestwood High School. These were exclusively African American public schools. Bells Mill Elementary was located at Bells Mill Road and Alexander Lane and is now the site of beautiful homes. As mentioned earlier, we only had two buses that picked up children. Bus 5 picked up the students that lived in Dawson Town, and bus 4 picked up the students that lived in Greenbrier Farms, Oak Grove, and Queen City. In elementary school, I was in the band playing the clarinet. My good friend Rodney Ricks whom I haven't seen since elementary school played the drums. I remember Elliot Lawson, who played the trumpet. Man, that was a long time ago! I was reared with the belief that White people were somehow superior and more intelligent than Blacks. My mother and grandmother always talked about having a White doctor and a White lawyer. I had never dealt directly with those of the opposite race, and the only experience I had in my childhood was that of dealing with the racist folk that drove through our community throwing bricks and rocks and calling us "Nigger, Nigger, Nigger."

So, here's what it was like for me as I came to understand what Dr. Martin Luther King, Jr. meant as he stood with other Blacks and sang the lyrics of "We Shall Overcome," which includes the line "Black and White together someday." After attending exclusively Black public schools from first through tenth grade, due to rezoning, I transferred to an integrated public school, Great Bridge High. And, unfortunately, Great Bridge High School is where some of those same Whites that raided our community attended school.

I remember my mom going to work early in the morning. I had to get up early with her and take my bath using a #2-foot tub. Then, we would walk out the door heading down Luther Street to 901 Bells Mill Road to my Cousins Cecil & Charlotte (Cousin Buster & Cousin Lottie) Bell. I remember walking into the house half asleep hearing every morning on the radio in their bedroom the song, "May the Work I've Done Speak for Me." Cousin Lottie would get a pillow and a blanket, and I would lie down on their burgundy leather sofa, and there I would sleep until it was time to catch the school bus. This was during the time I was attending Crestwood Junior High School in the 7th and 8th grades. I remember a few mornings that I barely caught the bus. I can see myself running down to the next bus stop to catch our school bus, Bus #84, driven by Mrs. Hattie Griffin.

Moving to the seventh grade (junior high) was different. New faces, several teachers (I could barely deal with one), and a ride on a school bus outside of Bells Mill. I had walked to school for six years, and now I'm catching Bus #84 with Mrs. Hattie Griffin as the driver. Couldn't do wrong because she knew Sweetie, and I knew Sweetie. Still, I saw only Black faces at Crestwood Junior High. Next, I went to high school in the ninth and tenth grades at Crestwood High. There were more Black faces as students, but we dealt with some white teachers for the first time. Mr. Hardee, who would later become the principal of Deep Creek High, Mr. Bloomfield, Mrs. Byrd, Mrs. Trimyer, Mrs. Duffy, and others.

In those days, we had community fights, such as Bells Mill against Crestwood or Gilmerton against Fentress. And there were community rules. For example, it was against the Crestwood rules for me to walk in the Crestwood community because I lived in Bells Mill. So, one particular day during school, the fellows from the Crestwood community and the Bells Mill community had been verbally antagonizing each other. After school, while we were all gathered on the bus ramp, waiting for our bus, Bus #84, to take us home, the fellows from the Crestwood community ran home and came back with sawed-off shotguns. They stood in the schoolyard about fifty yards away, pointing their guns at those of us waiting to get on the bus. I heard the fellows from Bells Mill saying, "Let the girls get on the bus first." I was the second one on the bus, and I'm not ashamed.

Despite the community situations like this, Crestwood High School was indeed a great school, both academically and athletically. The graduation rate was very high. I remember long before I attended Crestwood High, sitting in the bleachers watching the graduation ceremonies held on the football field. So many of my family members graduated from this prestigious high school. For the graduation ceremony, the female graduates wore white caps and gowns, white shoes, and stockings, accessorized by a pearl necklace with matching pearl earrings. The male graduates wore black caps and gowns, white dress shirts, black neckties, black pants, and black shoes that were so shiny you could see your face in them. Picture two long rows of students, females first, then the males. I can still see those graduates marching proudly in step to "Pomp and Circumstance," as it was played by the school band. They marched down the field and then turned, facing each other, still remaining in step to the music. Then, the administrators and teachers marched in sync between the two rows of students. They wore black caps and gowns with stoles draped around their neck, the color comparable to their field of study in college. Man, what a sight! After the teachers marched to their seats, the students turned simultaneously and marched down the field to the fifty-yard line where their chairs were neatly placed.

I was so disappointed when I graduated from a high school that did not embody ceremonial protocol nor demonstrate the high expectations from students as did my "almost" Alma Mater, Crestwood High School. Instead, I found myself in a free-for-all atmosphere at the school from which I eventually graduated, Great Bridge High School. When my graduating class walked on the field, that's exactly what everyone did, "walked" as if they were in the mall, waving to family and friends in the bleachers. No rhythm, no live band, but a tape played through the stadium intercom system. What a colossal mess.

At Crestwood High, I remember a fellow playing the piano in the auditorium for all the assemblies and how it affected my idea of what music should sound like. I can see him now playing the new hit song of the 70's era, "O Happy Day." I remember saying, "Man, I wish I could play like him." It was about this time that I began playing with Sis. Rosa Worlds and when God started developing His gift which He had given to me.

After being in the ninth and tenth grade at Crestwood High School, the school board decided to close or phase out our all-Black school. There was protest from the students. One day, the students walked out of school and marched from Crestwood High School to the school administration building on Cedar Road, located in Great Bridge. I must confess that I didn't march because I had a mother who would have marched a belt "on my behind" for leaving school. I recall some of the students I labeled "Big Shot Students" as we assembled in the school's stadium for a protest rally. These guys were Levi Willis (now a Bishop in the Church of God in Christ) and Barnard Jarvis, a very popular and outspoken student. He had the vocabulary of a lawyer. He was a great orator. When he would speak, we would respond loudly, screaming, and I would say to myself, "What the heck is he talking about." Well, what he was saying sounded good anyway.

All our marching and all of our protesting, and all of our speeches, were in vain. The "White powers that be" closed Crestwood High School, the all-Black school in Chesapeake, Virginia, the home of the fighting "Bombers." Students were sent to predominately White schools throughout Chesapeake: Deep Creek High, Indian River High, Western Branch High, Oscar Smith High, and then there was the home of the Wildcats, Great Bridge High School, where I was sent.

Crestwood High School is now Crestwood Middle School, the same building with the same halls. When I worked at the Transportation Department of Chesapeake Public Schools, I would drive my tire truck down the street to the old Crestwood High School stadium and walk around the track, walking and talking to God. Many times, my mind went back to the old days of the Friday night football games and the excellent commencements ceremonies that were held on the same track and field I was walking on. One day I remember standing on the fifty-yard line of the football Crestwood High School football field. I looked at both goal posts and observed how far they were apart. I also figured if I had been on the football team, I probably would have run to the wrong goal post. As I walked off the empty field, I said to myself, "Football players must be crazy. That's just too much running."

Crestwood High School was an extraordinary school. I have so many fond memories of the one year I attended. When I was a freshman, I liked my gym class playing basketball, and having fun, but I hated the week of "gymnastics." We had to do all kinds of tumbling and climbing ropes and all kinds of crazy exercises. A voice spoke to me in my head and said, "You've "NEVER" hooked class before, now is your time." So, when it came time to go to my gym class, something led me to go backstage in the auditorium. It was dark backstage with only the exit lights shining dimly on the step, but I stayed (hid-out) in this little area by myself, silently singing. Now, keep in mind, I had gym class in the morning, so it stood to reason when I didn't show up for class, Coach Williams (Rock) would notice. It also stood to reason that I would eventually see him in the hall at some time. So, a few days after missing gym class, while changing classes, I felt the firm grip of Coach Rock on my shoulder and heard what sounded like the voice of the Arch Angel saying, "Wilson, why were you not in class all week." Before I could answer with probably would have been a lie, I found myself in the office of Mr. Clifton Woods, the principal.

I tried to distract Mr. Woods by talking about the recent discovery that I had three siblings as this new information was the highlight of my life at the time. Mr. Woods requested that my mom come and visit him, who I considered the "un-merciful Queen Sweetie," known for her painful punishments. He explained to my mom that I had cut class. He continued by explaining to her that since I had never done this before, it was probably a stage I was going through because of the psychological things I was going through upon learning about my new siblings. If you know anything about the Favor of God, all I can say about this situation is, "FAVOR!" I took it to be the mercy of God, and I accepted what he said. It sounded good to me. However, I never cut class again.

September 1971, I found myself entering a school that I didn't want to attend. Crestwood High School was no more! My friends and I were tossed into a school with White kids who didn't want us there. The principal was Mr. Harry Blevins, whom I found out that my mom had worked at his home years ago as a domestic worker. Mr. James Calhoun was the assistant principal. In my opinion, to ensure that we Black kids "acted" like we were supposed to, Coach St. Clair Jones, a well-respected, probably 400-pound transfer-teacher from Crestwood High, was appointed as the assistant to the assistant principal. Smart move on their part because we all respected, no, we "FEARED" the man.

Due to integration, all of us students from Bells Mill found ourselves at Great Bridge High School. The only interaction I had ever had with White folk was their bottle-throwing, brick-throwing, head-slapping, name-calling display of racial animus towards those who didn't look like them. Of course, we were all aware of the activities of the Ku Klux Klan, who, according to rumors, held meetings in the fields off Johnstown Road and Washington Drive located off of Waters Road, where our church is now located.

As a result of integration and negative feelings between Black and White students, I witnessed many fights. Most of them, not all of them, didn't want us at Great Bridge High, and none of us that I knew of wanted to be there. Our hearts belonged to Crestwood. I remember the day I was on my way to class when I noticed the windows were open. Due to the cool of the autumn season, some of the Black students began closing the windows, and oh my God. When it was all said and done, school desks were hanging from the windows, and Black and White kids were "at it" like Batman and the Joker's men.

I remember walking the halls of Great Bridge High one day with a friend of mine from Bells Mill named Clifton (Bunky) Peterson. Like many of us, he was unhappy about being at Great Bridge High, and he showed it. As we walked down the hall, he took off his belt and whipped a White boy like a father punishing his own son. When Coach St. Clair Jones came walking down the hall, the fight broke up, and everybody just walked off as if nothing had happened.

I remember another incident that occurred in one of my classes. A White boy named Ronnie Edwards made it known that he did not care for people of color. This boy would sit behind me and kick my chair, continuously saying, "Hey nigger boy, hey nigger." I did not respond to his taunting because of my experiences with White Klansmen in Bells Mill and my lack of interaction with Whites.

I would love to lay hands on that young man now in "my name" (just kidding).

One of my favorite classes at Great Bridge High School was my Air Force ROTC class. I had taken ROTC at Crestwood High during my freshman and sophomore years, and now I was seriously taking the class at Great Bridge. In my senior year, I was a Lieutenant Major in the ROTC. I had fellows under my command. A White fellow named Charles Ketchum, whom we called Chuck, had a problem with this me, a Black guy being in charge. As the months went by, we grew closer as friends. It got to the place where we would call each other on the phone about ROTC projects. One day Chuck told me reluctantly, "Big Ed if you call my house and my dad answers the phone, please just hang up the phone." I didn't really understand his statement, so I questioned him. I said, "Why man, what's up?" He told me that his dad did not like "colored" people. I guess his dad recognized my voice as a black kid. That's when I understood why Chuck didn't care for me as a person. He was raised in a home that knew nothing but hatred towards people of color. Nevertheless, we became very close friends to the point that when I saw him several years later, he informed me he was about to get married and extended the honorable invitation to be the best man at his wedding. Though extremely honored, due to a prior obligation, I had to decline the invitation.

During my high school days at Great Bridge High, God blessed me to develop my own style of music. In the eleventh grade, I became the organist for a church down in a part of Virginia Beach known as Blackwater, mentioned in the earlier chapter titled "Over My Head, I Hear Music in the Air." In June or 1973, I graduated from Great Bridge High School with "Honors." Not the kind of honors one receives because of academic excellence but honored that I was getting the heck out of Great Bridge High School. My grades weren't that great. The only "A" I can remember getting was on the "A" in the absentee book for being absent. I must confess I was a "C, D, B" student. I now understand that the "C, D, B" probably stood for "Could've" Done "Better."

After graduating from Great Bridge High, the question I asked myself was, "What am I going to do next?" The Viet Nam war was going on, and sadly, two fellows who grew up in Bells Mill were killed when they stepped on a mine. So, I knew the military was not an option. So instead, I decided to go on to college and be somebody. Norfolk State College (now Norfolk State University) would be my next destination in life where, as already mentioned, I carried my God-given gift of playing gospel music with me.

After graduating from Great Bridge High School, I spent the summer working at the Chesapeake Social Services Department through the organization, Supporting Transformational Opportunities for People, better known as the STOP program. My job entailed delivering packages and destroying private documents, as well as washing city vehicles. I loved cleaning the city cars because it allowed me the privilege of driving cars without a license.

I had no idea what the future held for me. I knew the armed forces was not an option, although I had considered the Air Force because of my ROTC experience in high school. I just figured I would go on to college and see what happens and off I went to Norfolk State.

# 16.

# MY FUTURE WAS DOWNSTAIRS IN THE PING PONG ROOM

In September of 1973, I enrolled at Norfolk State College (now Norfolk State University). I had no idea what my major should be. As a matter of fact, I had never talked with my high school counselor because I felt, during the change from segregation to integration, the school didn't care about the folk of color. Maybe I was just too ignorant to know that I could confide in a school counselor concerning my future. I didn't know what a major or a minor was in college. After discovering what it meant to have a major, I decided to major in social work simply because I had worked that previous summer for the Chesapeake Social Service Department. I completed one semester in social work studies taking introductory courses. I soon discovered that college was a lot different than high school. If you didn't want to go to class, you didn't have to go. I would go up in the Student Union Building in the student lounge and watch television.

There were friends from my community and high school that were there also. We made connections with some other kids from Portsmouth and hung out with them in the student lounge. In the winter months, we actually had snowball fights in the lounge. We would go out to the balcony and grab some snow and act like, what I guess we were, kids. Of course, most of us had three things in common. We were all raised in the church, we all loved to fellowship and have fun, and we all loved gospel music and singing. One day the word got out that "Peterman" could play the piano. So, we found a piano upstairs in what was called Tidewater Hall, now Brown Hall. There was a piano in the lecture room upstairs in the elbow section where the halls met. Around lunchtime, we would go to Brown Hall and sing while Robbie Savage directed the group. We soon had students dropping in listening while doing homework or just being curious. Some of them soon joined us. We formed a gospel group on campus and named them the Black Inspirational Singers of Norfolk State. We soon felt that the name sounded too militant, so we changed the name to the Gospel Inspirational singers of Norfolk State. We didn't have a lot of singing engagements, but we sang when we could at programs on campus which consisted of other gospel groups.

At Norfolk State, I learned the meaning of an interesting, nice sounding word. I've always been quiet when serious conversations were occurring because I had low self-esteem, but when it came to "cutting up," that was right down my alley. I would cut up in class, causing my classmates to laugh at my behavior. One day one of my teachers said to me, "Mr. Wilson, you are a very 'loquacious' individual." Sounded good to me, so I responded, "Thank you." Her response to me was, "Look up the word." I did. Then, I kept quiet.

Next semester, I decided to change my major to music because of my love of music, piano playing, and organ playing. I had very little music training and had never completed the beginners' music book. And here I am, changing my major to music. This change resulted in me collecting my paperwork from the social services department head to take to the music department head. Then, I had to go to "some" professor's studio and sing to demonstrate my ear for music. I don't remember the professor's name, however, the name I remember and the person I admired was Professor Earnest

Brown. When I went to his studio for what I would call an audition playing the piano, Professor Brown gave me a hymn book. He turned to a page and told me to play the hymn. I looked at the book, looked at him, looked at the piano, and looked at him again and said, "I can't play this hymn, I can't read music." Professor Brown told me to play anything I wanted to play. I chose to play "Thank You, Lord." Professor Brown was so impressed. He said to me, "You can make it in this department if you have the will to do it. You play like you've been playing for years." I changed my major to music. I became good friends with Professor Brown. He called me "Pete." I remember Professor Brown was the minister of music at First Baptist Church Lamberts Point. He heard my group, The Gospel Inspirational Singers of Norfolk State College, sing on campus. The group sang the song by Rev. James Cleveland, "I Did It God's Way." This was a rearrangement of Frank Sinatra's "I Did It My Way." Professor Brown called me to his studio on campus and asked me to teach him the song. He wanted to teach it to his choir at First Baptist Lamberts Point. That next week he said to me, "Pete, we sang the song, and the folks were jumping the pews and swinging by the chandeliers," as he plucked his fingers.

The class I hated most was my piano class. My beginners' music book reminded me of something my grandchildren might use in a beginner's piano class. I would end the assigned "little kiddy song" during piano class by jazzing it up at the end. Mrs. Phelps, my piano teacher, would get angry and say, "Mr. Wilson, that's not in the book." My favorite class was my music theory class. I learned so much about music that has helped me to this day. I was supposed to give up playing by ear, the gift that God gave me, and concentrate on reading sheet music, but I couldn't do that. My unwillingness to learn how to read music worked against me as a music major at Norfolk State. Nevertheless, I advanced in my God-given musical gift as I learned so much by observing and listening to other music majors. I'd be in the practice halls hearing

THE THINGS I REMEMBER

these guys play, and they would see me and say, "Come on in Peterman." These were some of the nicest guys you'd ever want to meet. They would show me cords, and I learned a lot. While our lifestyles were different (they practiced an "alternative lifestyle"), we had mutual respect. I didn't finish college, but I was blessed to learn so much about music.

Music was and still is my passion. However, I remember some of what I learned in other classes. I had a history teacher named Dr. Rhodes who was so much into history that she would get excited and say, "Isn't this interesting?" I would respond to myself unChristian-like, "Hell no." I now find myself loving history, especially the history of the civil rights era and the history of past presidents. I loved my English class because I loved writing stories, which is why I'm doing this autobiography (boring you to life, hoping that you will lie and tell me how interesting it is). I have spent many days alone at Norfolk State, standing out on the balcony of the student union building, praying, and wondering what my future would be. I often wondered who I would spend my life with as a wife. I often wondered who would be the mother of my children and how they would look. I had no idea that the answer was downstairs in the ping pong room.

I used to catch a ride with Alfred Foreman Jr., who was my best friend at that time. Alfred loved to play ping pong down in the student union building. I would go there waiting to catch him home. This girl was with such a beautiful face and a big afro, pretty lips, a beautiful body, and lovely eyes. I dared not to even speak to this chick. I was an old country boy from Bells Mill, and she seemed to me to be "TOO" foxy to even me even the time of day. I had no idea that a few years later, this beautiful, wonderful, sexy, lovely fine young lady would not only give me the time of day, but she would give me her phone number and what I needed in my life, her hand in marriage. She would give me love, happiness, encouragement, her life, her loyalty, my children and become my inspiration

## MY FUTURE WAS DOWNSTAIRS IN THE PING PONG ROOM

and best friend. My future was waiting for me downstairs in the student union building playing ping pong.

As I mentioned in a previous chapter, there was another time when I was upstairs in the sanctuary of Trinity A.M.E. Church in the Berkley section of Norfolk, Virginia, and my future was downstairs in another rehearsal. I can't believe she actually came upstairs when she heard me playing the organ all by myself and watched me for a few minutes, and then she went back downstairs. I never knew this until years after we were married, and my wife told me of the incident. I remembered being there. Her name: Teresa Lynn Hill from Sunrise Hill. That's where I found "my thrill." My God, how I'm so grateful that God knew who and what I needed to make my life complete. In chapter eighteen, you will hear more about this angel sent from above. She was signed, sealed, and delivered to me. My answer to prayer, the mother of my children, the daughter my mother never had, and a most valuable part of the various ministries God has blessed me to work with for over fifty years. My supporter, encourager, prayer partner, lover, and best friend is Teresa Lynn (Tesee) Hill.

Teresa has always been my greatest supporter and a faithful encourager. There have been many times when I would have a hard time learning certain songs on the piano, and my wife would always encourage me that I could do it, and I did. Over the years, when I didn't feel like going to rehearsals, she always encouraged me to go, and she was always with me. Every choir I've played for in every church, she was a part of giving full support with that powerful anointed alto voice. She has been noted as being a singing alto section all by herself. My wife has never complained about all my traveling as minister of music for various churches and groups. I praise God for her being in my life and being an essential part of my music ministry over the years.

Even today, in our retirement years, she supports and encourages me in both the music and the preaching ministries that God has placed on my life. She is now a preacher of the gospel. So many people don't know it, but Teresa has a dynamic gift of studying and expounding on the word of God. She is a great teacher. She goes deep in her study of the Word of God, and she explains it with such clarity. I'm so proud of her! I praise God for choosing me to be hers and for choosing her to be mine. She is a woman of virtue and a woman of faith. She is so beautiful in spirit, mind, character, and body. I'm a blessed man. Better than blessed. I don't know what she sees in this old country boy from Bells Mill, but I'm so glad she sees it.

## 17

# WELCOME TO THE REAL WORLD OF WORKING

After two semesters at Norfolk State, I withdrew to work and help my mother with the bills. To be honest with you, my grades were not what they should have been because of my lack of studying. Nevertheless, I landed a job working for the Chesapeake Public Works Department, which lasted for about three years, from age nineteen to twenty-two. I worked with several crews on this job.

As a part of the gravel crew, we hauled tons of gravel to various neighborhoods and filled in people's driveways. Many in the Black community had no idea the city was responsible for their driveway from the edge of the road to where the telegram pole ended in their yards, about six and a half feet. The White folks would call the Public Works Department and say that their driveway was low in gravel. We would then go out and fill in their driveway. Not only that, but the Whites knew if they had a big or small ditch in front of their home and they wanted it to be filled in with dirt and landscaped, all they had to do was buy the pipes to go in the ditch and call Public Works. We would lay the pipes in the ditch, connecting them at the joints with concrete. Then we would haul in dump truck loads of soil or dirt and fill the piped ditch. In a community in the Great Bridge area, there is a home which I landscaped

## THE THINGS I REMEMBER

myself. After landscaping, the grass seeds had been planted, and there stood a beautifully landscaped yard from the road to the house with no ditch.

Another thing that the Black community did not know was they could call the city to get leaves out of their ditches because the leaves blocked the drainage. A lot of homes in Brentwood and Western Branch had many trees in the yard. When the leaves would fall from the trees, the white folk would rake the leaves in the ditch in front of their home and call the city to say the drainage was blocked back leaves in the ditch. I remember the big truck we used with a large vacuum hose on the end. We would put the vacuum hose down in the ditch, which was about twelve inches in diameter, and suck up the leaves only to get a call the next week to come back to the same home and do it again.

I worked on several crews with the city: asphalt, gravel, concrete, a flagman, broom tractor driver, dump truck driver, and so on. One of my favorite jobs was using the fifty-pound jackhammer to break up concrete. What a way to build up your body. I also drove the dump truck prisoners from prison local camp on the back of my truck in a small woodshed mounted on the back of my truck. I would drive my passengers, along with the foreman and the sheriff's deputy, with his rifle to various locations wherein they would clean out ditches. After dropping off the ten men, the sheriff deputy, and the foreman, I would take the two trustee prisoners to another location and pick up the dirt the prisoners had thrown on the shoulder of the road, cleaning ditches. The two trustees only had a few more months to serve in prison before being released. They were nice guys.

One day, my supervisor asked me to train a coworker on how to operate the dump truck. The trainee was a fellow from Bells Mill, named Lathan Blount, fondly known to us in Bells Mill as" Mutt." All the dump trucks left the yard at the same time. As we left the yard, I allowed Mutt to drive the truck. I had complained about some play in my steering wheel, but nothing was done to correct the situation. Mutt couldn't manage the movement in the steering wheel as well as I could. We left the yard with the other dump trucks loaded with tons of gravel. Mutt drove, and another young worker sat in the middle. I was on the truck's passenger side. My cousin Don Eason was about two trucks behind us as we traveled down Kempsville Road, approaching Battlefield Boulevard and Clearfield Avenue.

The vehicle was swaying from side to side, and I noticed it right away. Mutt did his best but was unable to catch the swerve. Suddenly, the truck began to flip over and over and over. I was told by my cousin Don that the dump truck flipped over three times. I remember bending over towards the dashboard. My radio was behind me in the truck with the song playing, "I'm blessed, I'm blessed, as I look around me, I realize I'm blessed." I'll never forget that moment. I remember closing my eyes, then looking up, I saw the ground upside down.

When the truck stopped rolling, it was facing the opposite direction on the opposite side of the street. We had landed in a big ditch. The truck was tilted, and I was leaning towards the ditch. The fellow beside me panicked and crawled over Mutt and jumped out of the broken driver's window. Mutt opened the door and climbed out. I was in shock, but I remember the truck was still running. Even though I had not accepted the call to preach at the time, the fellows called me "Preacher." I heard somebody screaming, "Preacher, get out of that truck before it blows up." I reached up and turned off the truck, then opened my door, which caused me to slide down into the ditch. I remember my radio falling into the ditch. As I climbed out of the ditch, I saw gravel all over the street.

The truck hit a telegram pole and knocked out the lights in the area. When I looked up, I saw the other trucks had stopped. Fellows were running to check on us. The first one to reach me was my cousin Don Eason, who picked up my Bible lying in the middle

THE THINGS I REMEMBER

of the street. Don said, "Are you ok, Pete?" The ambulance came and rushed the three of us to the hospital. Then I was returned to my workplace. I got my first glimpse of the vehicle. The cab had been smashed. Instead of being pushed in, the windshield had been pushed out. Our supervisor knew that someone was either hurt or dead. Praise God: even then, God had His angels to protect us. Mutt and the other young fellow quit the job after a few weeks and "never" came back to work.

I was working with the city when I met the love of my life, Teresa. I had bought my first car, which was a powder blue 1968 Custom Ford. I later got my second car, a burgundy 1975 LTD. That car was sweet. At this time, Teresa was driving a Volkswagen station wagon. I remember I used to carpool with five men. It was in the wintertime, and my girlfriend needed some money. I met her in front of Roses near Battlefield Boulevard and Military Highway. My beautiful girlfriend drove up in the Volkswagen with gloves on and wrapped up in a coat, scarf, and skull cap. There was no heat in her car, and she was freezing. It hurt my heart to see this, so I gave her my LTD to use, and I took her no heated car and drove it until we got it fixed. The men were not happy, but who cared? Finally, one day this old man named Mr. Albert Jones asked me, "Are you crazy?" I said, "Hell yea!"

I enjoyed working for Public Works with two years at the Bowers Hill station and one year at the Butts Road station. I knew this was not the job for me and that I needed to better myself. After leaving Public Works, Mr. Oliver Jacobs, the owner and manager of Oliver Jacobs Construction Company, offered me a job. Mr. Jacobs offered me a temporary position until I could find a better one. Actually, I didn't do too much. I assisted in the excavation of foundations for dwellings for which he poured concrete. I'd go on runs for him and do everything he asked. His main worry was that I do not injure my "piano" fingers.

# WELCOME TO THE REAL WORLD OF WORKING

One night Mr. Jacobs invited Teresa and me to his home to sing for his guests. Mr. and Mrs. Jacobs had a big, beautiful home on Waters Road, complete with a piano, an organ, a pool table, and a large aquarium built into his living room wall. They also had an in-ground pool that I had helped to cover with a fiberglass house.

As we worked in Virginia Beach, laying the foundation for some homes behind the Haynes Furniture store, I went to Haynes to use the payphone to call my girlfriend, Teresa. While in Haynes, I completed a job application, and I got the job. God allowed me to work at Haynes, and I became a husband to my sweetheart Tesee. Working there allowed me to furnish our apartment with furniture, carpeting, and other needs for our home. It has been said that we had the "Baddest" apartment in Harbor North at 1174 Harbor Place. I praise God for mapping out a plan for my life with this wonderful, beautiful, sexy, intelligent, wise, loving, cooking, spirit-filled woman Teresa Lynn Hill, My wife for life and the mother of my children.

# 18.

# THE TIRE MAN AT CHESAPEAKE PUBLIC SCHOOLS

In August 1984, I was employed with the Chesapeake Public Schools Transportation Department as a mechanic helper. I never understood the title because I didn't help mechanics. My job was to service school buses by changing the oil and filters, fuel filters, checking fluid levers, and mainly changing and preparing school bus, truck and car tires, and lawn equipment such as lawn-mowers, tractors, and carry trailers. Before the department got a tire changing machine, I was responsible for breaking down and putting back together twenty school bus tires at a time with a tire hammer and two tire bars. This task was a lot of physical work, and I felt mighty good doing it for exercise and, of course, for the money to feed my family. In the last ten or twelve years of working there at the transportation department, I was totally in charge of all tire inventory. I still had my tire truck which I drove home each night if a bus had a flat tire after hours. My first tire truck was #373. Then I got a brand-new truck, #453. Over the thirty-one years that I worked at the transportation department, I had a few close calls.

I can recall several tires exploding, nearly costing me my life. Once on a road call, I was inflating the tire on a bus to raise it to get the hydraulic jack under the axle, and the tire exploded on the side facing the bus's engine. I was standing on the outside of the tire. It was so loud it sounded like a cannon, and the air's impact knocked some parts off the engine. My supervisor sent a mechanic (Fred Albergotte) to check on me, believing I was seriously injured. If the tire had exploded on the outside where I was standing, I wouldn't be here writing this book. I prayed and thanked God for His grace and mercy.

Another incident occurred when I returned from lunch and discovered that my helper had left for me to repair. My helper at the time (James Trent) had dismounted the tire off the truck and was on his way to lunch as I returned from lunch. I rolled the tire to the tire machine and walked away to put my lunch box and my book down when the tire just blew up out of nowhere. I had taken about three or four steps when it happened. I would not be writing this book if I had worked on the tire immediately and not walked away. I prayed and thanked God for His grace and mercy.

One last situation I want to mention happened as I was working on a tire. Suddenly, as I was working on the tire, it exploded within a couple of feet from my face. It was so loud that the guys outside came running in, asking was I ok. The people in the front office heard it and thought the bus had fallen off a lift. As the mechanics came running to me, the impact frightened me so bad I fell back. As the fellows talked to me, asking if I was ok, their voices sounded like cartoon characters, as if they had plastic over their mouths. This incident occurred in 2001, and I continue to suffer from a loud ringing in my right ear, which necessitates my watching television while listening to music to distract myself from hearing the ringing. Nevertheless, "I AM HEALED!" God blessed me with safety all those years working on tires. Yes, I had a few very close calls "But God!"

Those thirty-one years of working at Chesapeake were filled with more good days than bad days. God blessed me to gain many wonderful friends at the transportation department. I got the job

## THE TIRE MAN AT CHESAPEAKE PUBLIC SCHOOLS

through my friend, Pastor O. L. Cromwell II, who had become the pastor of New Oak Grove Baptist Church in the Blackwater section of Virginia Beach, Virginia, where I was the church's minister of music for the young adult choir. I had been there about six years before Pastor Cromwell came. He was also a school bus mechanic at Chesapeake Public Schools. I needed a job to take care of my wife and children, and he put in a word for me. We had a good time working and laughing together as we spent each day making sure the buses were safe for the children. In my years of working for the transportation department, I saw many guys come and go.

I remember the days of planting Bibles in the bathroom for the fellows and me to read. I put a Bible in each bathroom stall, and when they would disappear, I would be happy believing that somebody was reading them. I tried to carry myself respectably all though I missed the mark sometimes. I mean, there were a few guys who could get under my skin. One day, an older fellow named Kermit Capps informed the foreman that I was stealing gas. I was running late that morning, so I went directly to the garage instead of fueling up. Then I received a tire call in Western Branch. I knew I didn't have enough fuel to go there and back, so I quickly fueled my truck, intending to fill out the fuel book when I got back. It was important to get the tire replaced on the bus so the kids would get to school on time. When I got back, Mr. Joe Palmer, the shop foreman, informed me that Kermit had mentioned to him that I had filled up my truck and had not recorded it in the gas log. I explained what happened, and Mr. Palmer, knowing me as he did, said it was not a problem because he knew something had happened for me not to fill out the book. Then a voice spoke to me and said, "Go and find Kermit." When I found him, I blessed him in "my name" up and down. I said some things I was not proud of, and I "thought" some things as well. Needless to say, I went back to him and apologized, not for what I said but for the way I said it. After that, we never had another problem.

I would "lay" guys out using a few "choice" words unbecoming of a Christian. Then I would go back and apologize for my actions, always making sure I sent a strong message that they should leave me alone. But, as I said, in the end, I apologized for using words not appropriate for a Christian.

We would pull pranks on each other and joke on each other. If I were to start telling you some of the jokes we did and pranks we pulled, it would take up the whole book you're reading. So instead, I will mention a few to show you the kind of men who worked on the buses that you and your children probably rode to school. When I first started working with the Chesapeake Public Schools Transportation Department, I worked with an older man who was like a father to me named Mr. John W. Snipes. Mr. Snipes was a great prankster. One day, we listened to a nice but wild white guy named David, who can be described as sort of a hippy. He loved to curse and loved listening to the singer named Ozzy Osborne. It is reported that he bit the head off a bat at one of his concerts, not knowing that the bat was still alive.

One day David came in bragging about how he had side-swiped a car on the interstate the night before. He had this eight-cylinder Trans-am, and he loved to drive fast and radical. Well, the next day, Mr. Snipes came to work with a Polaroid and took some pictures. He took the pictures off the picture covers and threw the picture covers around David's Trans-am. It had rained the night before, so he made some footprints all around David's car. It just so happened that a state trooper dropped by the office concerning state inspections for the school buses. When David came back from a road call, Mr. Snipes told him that a state trooper had been by and looked around his car and saw the scratches on his car. David said, "You're lying, man." Mr. Snipes said, "Ed, didn't you see the state trooper?" I said, "Yes. sir, I did." If that wasn't good enough, Rev. O. L. Cromwell, a mechanic there at that time, came to our tire cage and confirmed seeing the state trooper there. We didn't

## THE TIRE MAN AT CHESAPEAKE PUBLIC SCHOOLS

lie. David went to investigate his car, and when he saw the footprints and Picture covers around his car, he knew that the trooper had been at his car taking pictures. David was afraid, and he was about to run to the time clock and clock out. We had to convince him that it was a prank.

Another prank pulled by Mr. Snipes was when he brought an old wallet to work and put a $10.00 bill halfway in it with a lot of it sticking out and showing. He then tied the wallet to a very long piece of sewing thread, and he laid the wallet in the middle of the garage floor. He then hid behind some tires and waited for someone to come by and attempt to pick up the wallet with the money in it. An old silly but nice man, Mr. Ron Ward, came walking by with that ugly walk he had, and when he saw the wallet with the money sticking out of it, he looked around to see who was looking. Mr. Ward didn't see Mr. Snipes, hiding behind the tires with the long string in his hand. When he bent down to pick up the wallet and get the money, Mr. Snipes swiftly pulled the wallet on the string as Mr. Ward proceeded to literally run, chasing the wallet.

Then there was the time when I borrowed or stole a white fellow named Dewey's work badge. I found a picture of Don King, the sports promoter, and made sure it was just the right size and I scotch taped it on Dewey's badge. He walked around all day with his badge showing his upper body and Don King's face unknowingly.

Another incident happened on a "very" hot summer day. The same mechanic named Mr. Ward, who was always playing practical jokes on everybody, came at me with the water hose, and he spayed me with it laughing. I told him I would get him back. He watched for me all day, knowing that I would do something to him. I had a large cup from Hardee's restaurant, and I filled it with ice and water. I snuck up behind him, pulled his t-shirt open, and poured that giant cup of ice water down his back. I felt terrible afterward because his behavior gave me the impression that he was experiencing a heart attack. He threw himself on the ground, laughing, and cursing at the same time.

This same man was sitting on his work stool with a rag hanging out of his back pocket, which he used to wipe his hands. He was working on a bus when I snuck up behind him without him knowing it, and I put a big blob of axle grease on the rag hanging from his pocket. I quietly folded the rag and stood up behind him. I then had a little bit of axle grease in the center of my hand. I said, "What's up, Mr. Ward?" as I reached out to shake his hand. He shook my hand and got the grease that was in my hand all over his hand. He said a few choice words laughing and reached for the rag in his back pocket. As he attempted to wipe his hands off, he smeared that big blob of grease that I put in his rag all over his hands. He said cuss words that I didn't even know existed.

Then there was the time that my friend, Leo McGroarty, planted old cameras up over my working area while I was at lunch. When I got back, the fellows told me that the administration had installed cameras to monitor our working (though years later, they really did). So, all that day and the next, I would do my work, and then I would sit down to rest, sometimes reading or eating a snack. Then, suddenly, I would remember that the boss was probably watching me through the camera. So, I would jump up and work with extra energy. Finally, after a day and a half, I was told by the fellows that the camera looking down at me was a dummy camera planted by Leo.

These were the types of practical jokes that went on from year to year as guys came and left. These were such good fellows to work with. During my time at the transportation department, I had some good partners working with me in the tire cage. Such partners included Chuck Carr, James Trent, James Cope, and Joshua Snell. Others included Anthony Foreman, a member of the young adult choir from New Oak Grove, where I served as the minister of music. When I started playing for New Oak Grove, Anthony

## THE TIRE MAN AT CHESAPEAKE PUBLIC SCHOOLS

was still a young boy. And then there was my Christian buddy, Rob Mobley. He became a prayer partner with me as we shared our faith. Rob, who is White, once told me jokingly about a Black family that visited his church. He said that the family was enjoying themselves until the choir, who was *all* dressed in white, came out wearing white robes. He said he never saw the family again. Man, that was funny! The last partner or helper I had was a young man who became like a son to me. A young, very smart twenty-one-year-old White boy named Joshua Snell. Josh and I got along really well as I attempted to help him grow spiritually. We had many talks about God and faith. I really tried to let my light shine on the job, talking to the fellows whom I loved, giving them Bibles and literature on the things of God. Some guys I had serious counseling with, not giving them my opinion but what the word of God had to say about their situation. Don't get it twisted, I was no saint. There were days when I needed counseling myself because I was ready to go "upside" somebody's head because sometimes folk just get on your nerves. No, I wasn't perfect, but I tried to live a life that demonstrated my love for God, and because of the life I lived, all the guys respected me in a special way. During rough times I had friends sent by God, like Vernon Jones, who came by to encourage me.

During the first ten years of working in the transportation department, I received a request. Mr. Donald Travitz, the shop superintendent, asked me if I would dress as Santa Clause for the mechanic's Christmas party. I agreed to do it. I guess he selected me because I was the tallest and biggest guy there at the shop. You have to understand, Mr. Travitz was a strict boss who didn't play and was always serious about things. Well, the day of the party came, and he paged me to come to his office. When I got to his office, he gave me this Santa outfit to put on. It fit me nicely. I had the red coat and pants trimmed with white fur along with the Santa had and beard. I saw a side of Mr. Travitz that I had never seen before. He was just like a little kid clapping his hands and saying, "Ed, that's great, oh my, you look good, let's go and see the fellows, this is great." I wouldn't have been surprised if I had gotten a raise for being Santa. The mechanics came into the mechanic lounge, and I came in with their gifts: a little yellow school bus piggy bank. I passed them out to each mechanic and gave my loud Santa laugh. One of the White wise crack mechanics named Steve laughed and said out loud, "Hey man, I thought Santa Clause was White." And he laughed, and he laughed. Being as silly as I am, I came back with a wisecrack comeback, "I don't care what the White man says, Santa Claus was Black!" Then I did my loud Santa laugh. The fellows fell out laughing. Steve said, "That was a good one, Ed."

One special person I have to mention is my supervisor Mr. Ed Godwin. Out of all the guys at the job, Ed has a special place in my heart because he was more of a brother than a boss. Whenever I needed help in any way, Mr. Godwin was always there. I dare not put him on the spot by mentioning how he was such a blessing to my family and me but let's just say he is (TRULY) a brother from another mother. Just like I knew I could depend on Ed, he knew he could depend on me. So, when guys didn't want to work overtime, I was there. My priority was to take care of my wife and my children, and Ed allowed me to work all the overtime I could, which helped him as well. He knew my heart.

Sometimes when Ed would get on my nerve about something, I would simply say sarcastically, "WHATEVER." I would say it to him so much until I wrote it on a piece of cardboard and stapled it to his bulletin board, and when I needed to, I would just point to the bulletin board and walk out of his office. To this day, even after I retired, when we contact each other, whether by call or by text, I will give him a "WHATEVER." Sometimes, he will text me and end the text by saying, "I know, WHATEVER," with a smiley face. Ed is a good man, and we have adopted him into our family. He loves my wife, my kids, and my grandkids. Ed and his wife

## THE TIRE MAN AT CHESAPEAKE PUBLIC SCHOOLS

attended my daughter Sherita's wedding, and they were with us when we gave my mom her last birthday celebration at her church five months before she passed away. Ed was with me and came to the funeral home when my mom passed away. He was with me at my church for my retirement celebration. Even today, if there is a need that my family and I have, I know he would be there to supply that need: William Edwin Godwin, my boss, my friend, my brother.

Years of picking up, breaking, changing, and lifting tires of all sizes took a toll on my body. (In the flesh, not in the spirit because I am healed). I developed arthritis in both knees and sciatic nerve in my back. I tried to endure the pain for two more years to retire with thirty-three years of service at the age of sixty-two, wherein I could draw social security, but the pain was too intense. It was hard to walk back and forth from my working area to the shop office and parts room. My buddy, Joshua Snell, and I started taking tire calls together because it was too difficult for me to do it alone. Finally, I had to go on a road call alone to a bus, and I climbed under the bus to place the jack lift under the axle. When I tried to get up, I couldn't. Finally, I kept trying until I made it up. I went back to the shop and told Ed that my time was up. I could no longer do my job for the pain. My wife had already discussed my well-being with me out of concern, but God had to show me that it was time to retire. I had worked at CPS Transportation Department from August 1984 until August 2015 through many dangers, toils, and snares. Nothing but the grace of Almighty God kept me.

On my last day of thirty-one years, it was like a dream. Mr. Godwin had instructed the night crew to come in on the day shift to share in my retirement gathering with the fellows. Various fellows got up to express remarks about me. I was quite honored because I had no idea that God had used me in such a way to inspire and encourage these guys with whom I had so much fun working with over the years. I think the most heartfelt moment were the words that came from my friend, Eric Person, whom I had known for so many years. I remember young Joshua Snell, my working partner, giving me a nice card and, in that card, he wrote a very nice, heartfelt note saying that I was the best partner he had ever worked with. Joshua was only about nineteen or twenty years old and had recently gotten married. In addition, he gave me a love token of a crisp one-hundred-dollar bill. That was very special. At three-thirty that evening, I loaded my belongings on the back of Joshua's pick-up truck (he lived near me in Deep Creek), and as we were pulling off to go home, I got a big surprise. My buddy Eric Person, the mechanic comedian of the shop, got into his road van, and my buddy Fred Albergotte escorted me home as I rode with Joshua. One drove in the front of us, and one drove behind us with their yellow-amber lights and emergency lights flashing. Eric called my wife and told her, "We're bringing him home." When we got to my house, Teresa was outside clapping and waiting. That was so special to me. I praise God for the great experiences and the many years of friendships I gained at the Chesapeake Public Schools Transportation Department.

# 19.

# I FOUND MY THRILL IN SUNRISE HILL

I served as an organist for many churches over the years. One of those churches was St. James AME church youth choir. It was with this choir that I found my thrill. The youth choir was very gifted in their singing ability. We would accompany the church's concert choir to their concerts by rendering three selections during the concert. On the first Sunday in December 1976, the concert choir gave a concert at the Mt. Zion Baptist Church in the Berkley section of Norfolk, Virginia. As the youth choir was singing, I observed this beautiful young lady in the audience looking at me with eyes that I felt calling my name. With her was a pretty little two or three-year-old baby.

I recognized her from somewhere. Didn't know where but I knew I had seen her before. That big soft-looking afro and those pretty soft-looking lips. She held her fingers to her chin, and I tell you, it really messed me up. It was that same beautiful chick I had seen in the ping pong room at Norfolk State. This fine, lovely, beautiful chick was looking at me, "Peterman," from Bells Mill, and you best to believe I was looking at her. God was painting a picture of the future for my life. She later told me that her best friend sitting beside her told her we'd better stop before we fell in love. After the concert, a lady came up to me and told me how much she enjoyed the choir. She also told me that her sister was interested in joining the choir. I asked who her sister was, and guess who she pointed to? That fine foxy chick. Her name was Teresa Lynn Hill, better known by her family as Tesee.

Sometime later, Teresa came to rehearsal at St. James to join the choir. That night I taught my arrangement of "I Must Tell Jesus." When the chorus part was sung, I heard this powerful alto voice that just blew my mind. I said, "Who is that singing like that?"

One of the girls responded, thinking I was talking about her, but I knew who it was. I got Teresa's phone number and began calling her. I couldn't believe this fine, beautiful young lady was giving me the time of day. We went out on our first date. I had to pick her up from a rehearsal she was having with another choir she sang with. It was a group directed by her aunt Mrs. Shirley Robertson called The Friendship Chorus. Another member of the St. James Youth choir was in the Friendship Chorus also. Her name was Marion Grant, and her father was the pastor of St. James AME Church.

Marion asked for a ride home. I had my first car, a 1968 Ford Custom 500. She (my car) was old, but she was clean. Teresa got in the car beside me as Marion sat at the window. When Marion got out of the car, Teresa started moving over, and I told her, "Stay where you are. Your seat is right here." From that day to this day, that's where Teresa has been, right beside me. Through thick and thin, she's been right beside me. In December of 1976, my friend and fellow musician William (Billy) Brown invited the St. James choir to his house for a Christmas party. Teresa was there looking unbelievably beautiful with that big soft afro. As she was about to leave, I walked her outside, picked her up, and turned her around. My goodness, I wanted her to be mine. God blessed us to be together.

Teresa and I were and still are together. We were together on many, many dates. We were together on November 25, 1978, when she became my wife. We were together from Elizabeth Courts Townhouses in Virginia Beach to Harbor North apartments, to Fernwood Farms, and Mill Creek (Deep Creek) all in the city of Chesapeake. We were together when her father and mother, Mr. Linwood & Mrs. Betty Hill, went home to be with the Lord. We were together when my father, Mr. Edward Marvin Ashby, went to be with the Lord. We were together when my mother, who lived with us for twenty-five years, passed away in our home. We are still together as we currently reside in our lovely, blessed apartment in Holly Point, located in the Georgetown section of Chesapeake. We are still together as we celebrate our children's adulthood, Keisha Lynn, Sherita Lakeisha, Ashley Chante', and Teresa Nicole. We're still together through sunshine and rain, heartaches and pain, ups and downs. Tesee, as a lot of folks call her, is my best friend, confidant, lover, encourager, prayer partner, and angel from above.

On November 25, 1978, we were married in New Central Baptist Church, my Tesee's home church. I remember the night before our wedding, my best friend at that time, Alfred Foreman Jr., and I were putting furniture together at the townhouse that Teresa and I were to move into, Elizabeth Court Townhomes, located three blocks from the beach in Virginia Beach. We were eating oranges and drinking sodas having a great time preparing for a night of beauty with the love of my life as we put the bedroom furniture together along with the other furniture for the other rooms. The best thing I could have done in life was to marry the love of my life on this important date of November 25, 1978. I remember I had purchased a yellow 1978 Ford Granada, and I had run around so much, I had forgotten to wash the car. Kevin Wilson (no relation), now Pastor Kevin Wilson, a member of St. James AME youth choir, took my car as I was in the church preparing to get married and ran it through a car wash for me. I remember Teresa walking down the aisle with that beautiful long wedding dress and that pretty hat pulled down to cover her beautiful face. I remember all I could see were those gorgeous, luscious lips painted with red lipstick. Teresa had not worn lipstick before, but it complemented her already natural beauty. I have always loved that my wife does not need lipstick or makeup, although she wears a little now.

I know we were ordained to be together. I've learned so much from my wife as a husband. She has been and still is a dream come true in my life. My wife supports everything I do as a husband, a musician, and a minister of the gospel. God has given her the ability to love everyone. She shows her love for others by continually encouraging and complimenting people. She has been and still is a counselor to many and a blessing to all that know her. I'm so glad God chose me for her and her for me. I love Teresa like Christ loves the church and gave his life for it. I would quickly lay down my life for this angel sent from heaven through the womb of Mrs. Betty Hill. I praise God for forty-three years of marriage, and prayerfully, by the time this book is published, it will be forty-three years. I am so grateful that her beautiful face is the first face I see in the morning and the last face I see at night. She is a beautiful, sexy, wise, caring, loving, total precious body of loveliness.

I say again, the greatest blessing of my life was the day I married Teresa Lynn Hill. There can be no greater love for a woman than I have for Tesee. I also know that she feels the same love for me. I praise God for a wife who loves me with unconditional love. Tesee is the most unselfish, sweetest, loving, friendliest person I know. Her beauty begins inside and travels outside to her beautiful body. People are drawn to her personality. I praise God for blessing me with the special "ANGEL" from above.

Now, my wife is sweet, but don't mess with her husband or her children. You'd rather be in a dog pit with pork chop draws on than to mess with her family. You'd rather run in a fire with gasoline-soaked pants on than mess with her family.

I thank God for Teresa's siblings, but one family member is near and dear to my heart. David Allen Hill, Teresa's brother, is my dearest friend. I remember the days that David, Pat (his wife), along with Teresa and me, would ride around during our courtship days looking at big beautiful homes and wondering what kind of money the homeowners made. We would double-date a lot and eat out a lot. There was and still is a special bond between us, as family and best friends. David and Pat got married one month after Teresa and me on December 23, 1978. Same church, same pastor, some of the same participants, it was like our wedding all over again.

I am blessed to have in my life my first child Keisha Lynn Wilson born on December 5, 1974, in Norfolk General Hospital. She was and still is a beautiful girl now married with three children of her own. Keisha being our first child, taught me how to be a dad. I love and forever will love her with all my heart. One of the greatest days of my life was the day my wife blessed me to be a father to my beautiful, sweet Kei Kei. I love my little baby, and to this day, she is the apple of my eye and a wonderful wife and mother. She blessed us with our first three grandchildren with her husband, whom I call my son, LaMans (Monzie) Fuller. A soft spoken and wise woman with a sweet personality and inward as well as outward beauty. Like all our daughters, she has the gift to sing and the gift of wisdom and knowledge.

On December 24, 1983, we were blessed to have our second daughter Sherita Lakeisha Wilson. Sherita was born in Virginia Beach General Hospital. I can still see her with those rosy cheeks and that pretty hair with the receding hairline. For a long time, Keisha thought that Sherita was her baby. I thought Sherita would be named Edward J. Wilson Jr., but God knew that a young man named Raynald David would one day need a helpmate in his life, so he gave us a Sherita and not an Edward Junior. From that marriage, I gained another son. Sherita is a math genius who is very sensitive and sweet in spirit. Like all our daughters, she is a beautiful woman of faith and has the gift of "ear" by way of singing. She looks like her daddy.

## THE THINGS I REMEMBER

Years later, on November 2, 1987, we were blessed with the birth of a baby girl whose Indian-like features accentuated her beauty (my great-great-grandmother was part Native American). We welcome our third daughter, Ashley Chante' Wilson, into the world. Ashley was born in Virginia Beach General Hospital also. I again thought a boy was coming. When she was born, I told the doctor, "Hey, something is missing." He said, "No sir, you have a baby girl." My Aunt Laura, and her daughters, Jackie, and Rona had just gotten to the hospital to bring me something to eat because I had been at the hospital all day. I remember running to the waiting room, sliding on the floor with those cloth shoes on, and saying, "It's another girl." I now had three beautiful, lovely daughters.

Eighteen months later, we found ourselves back at Virginia Beach General having our fourth and final baby. Teresa Nicole Wilson (Nikki) was born on March 6, 1989. I must share another testimony. When we were pregnant with Nikki, as we call her, the enemy tried to attack our spirit as well as our faith and family. One funny thing that happened is that the same nurse who assisted Teresa eighteen months earlier when Ashley was born was the same nurse that attended Teresa with the birth of Nikki. In both cases, I was dressed in a suit because we had been to church. In both cases, I asked to use a phone to call Billy Brown, a fellow musician, if I needed him to play for me. The nurse said, "Wait a minute, we've been through this before." She was right.

When my wife was pregnant with Nikki, the physicians were concerned with my wife's age at the time of this pregnancy. The doctors were also concerned about her blood results and wanted my wife to have an amniocentesis test. They were concerned that the baby would be Downe Syndrome. We were instructed to go to a counselor and discuss these special children's life expectancies and personalities. On the day my wife got the news, she came to my job to tell me, and she was very upset. I remember her with that soft pink turtleneck sweater on looking so beautiful and soft. It was on a Friday because we went to the church that David and Pat were attending called Word of Life Christian Center on Princess Anne Road in Virginia Beach for "Miracle Night Service."

Teresa and I went to the service that night. I remember I had on a brown suit, and my wife was in a maternity dress. I remember the altar call as I stood up in prayer for a miracle for my wife and our baby. After a good while, I heard this voice from the microphone saying, "You, in the brown suit. God is hearing your call. Come on down." As I walked to the front of the church towards Pastor Martin, he said, "Is it Will, Williams?" I replied, "Wilson." He said, "What is it that you need from the Lord tonight?" I had Teresa on my mind. I said, "I'm standing for my wife." Pastor Martin said, "We'll get to your wife, but what do you need?" I said, "Pray for my ministry." He prayed for me and told me to keep doing what I was doing in ministry. Then he said to me, "Go get your wife." As I proceeded to get Teresa, she was already walking towards the altar. As she approached, the tongue-speaking, faith-believing were prayer warriors, were already talking to God on her behalf, and I saw a light shining down like the glory of God! My wife began to spin around in circles praising God. He prayed for my wife and the baby inside her, and then he jumped back and said, "I see the enemy leaping from the womb." He then said, "The enemy seeks to take the child; don't go back the way you came." We came with hope, but we left with faith. We knew that God was in control, and we had peace that all was well with our baby.

Teresa and I went to Norfolk General Hospital to see a counselor prepared to counsel us on bringing a Down syndrome child into the world. The doctor asked us how we felt about aborting our baby, but we wouldn't hear of it. The young lady began showing us pictures of these special children, describing how they are sweet, loving children. We listened respectfully. My wife was sitting down as I walked back and forward with our newest baby Ashley in my arms. The young lady stopped and said to my wife, "You seem to be so calm and at peace with this. Other mothers would be upset and historical." My wife shared her testimony with the young lady, and I shared my testimony. We shared how we knew that whatever the problem was with our baby, all would be well. We believed and trusted God for a miracle.

She paused and made us promise to contact her when the baby was born. So, when Nikki was born, I made three phone calls; one was to my mother, one was to my mother-in-law, and the last was to the young lady, the counselor at Norfolk General Hospital who was preparing us to receive a Down syndrome baby. God had once again shown how great He really is. God has the power to change and rearrange things in our lives. He's a miracle worker. God had given us four wonderful, beautiful, brilliant, gifted daughters who would one day become God-fearing women. They all love singing, and my greatest joy is when they're all together laughing, singing, and reflecting on times past.

Keisha, our oldest daughter, and her husband Monzie have blessed us with three beautiful grandchildren: Ryan, Aayla, and Alaynah Fuller. I remember when Keisha was in middle school, she was asked to participate in a wedding. She was so excited. The Saturday before the wedding, I was cutting the grass in Fernwood Farms, where we lived. I was mowing the front yard as my wife watched from the front porch. Keisha was riding her bicycle. She was about to turn into our driveway when I heard my wife scream from the top of her lungs. I was pushing the loud lawnmower, and as I turned towards the street, I saw my daughter hit by a car. She rolled and hit the windshield, rolled down the car's hood, and hit the road. I immediately ran to her and picked her up. As I picked her up, her body went limp. The neighbor behind us, Mrs. Florence Walker, was in her backyard and saw the accident and called 911. God blessed us by allowing the paramedics to be two blocks away, looking at new houses being built. They responded and were there within a few minutes. My daughter was taken to the hospital, and all praise to God, the angels had softened her blow, and she had no broken bones and no scars. She had glass in her hair and was told that she would be really sore the next day. The next day on that Sunday, neighbors came to check on Keisha. We had a visit from Mr. George McCadden Sr., a prominent businessman in the Tidewater area, checking to make sure our baby was ok. There was no soreness. The only concern Keisha had was, "Can I still be in the wedding." The girl's father who hit Keisha checked on her, telling me that he knew there had to be a serious injury when he saw his daughter's car. To God be all the glory for his angels of protection and for allowing Keisha to become a beautiful mother of three beautiful children. She is a woman of wisdom and knowledge. She is a "go-getter" who constantly exudes the persona of the Proverb 31 woman, "She oversees the care of her house. She is never lazy" (27).

Our daughter Sherita and her husband Ray have blessed us with two grandchildren, Raynald David III and Rayah David. Sherita is a brilliant mathematician. This daughter teaches something that I can barely spell. She is a chemistry teacher at Woodrow Wilson High School in Portsmouth, Virginia. She is also the youth minister at our church, The Church of the Living God Center for Change, and is truly anointed to present the Word of God with clarity that reaches the young and the old.

Ashley Chante' Wilson is a beautiful Nubian princess. Her Native American complexion makes her a beauty to behold, and she is a walking "fashion statement." Though not yet discovered, she is a gifted fashion designer. Her fashions are traditional with a touch of elegance. Upon request, Ashley will uniquely design and manufacture anything from a pantsuit to a wedding gown. Her talents are well hidden to the public, but we, her family, know she is innovative, creative, and on the cutting edge of the future of fashion.

Teresa Nicole Wilson (Nikki), our baby, can only be described as the princess of glamour and God's gift to the world of vocal music. Her talents range from singing to teaching children to modeling. Whatever her hands are assigned to do, she does it well!

Teresa and I are exceedingly blessed. Yes, we have been down many times, but the ups far outweigh the downs. Here we are, almost 43 years later as one in the flesh, blessed with four uniquely beautiful and gifted adult daughters and five beautiful grandchildren. And while our girls are grown and on their own, my favorite time is when all my children and grandchildren come to dinner, and we just talk, laugh, and sing. My girls can really, really, sing! God continues to bless us as ministers of the gospel. He continues to bless me to serve as the pastor of music and media and Teresa as our church's praise and worship leader. God has taken us through many valleys, across many rivers, and over many mountains, but I can genuinely say that we are enjoying life, enjoying God, and enjoying each other.

## 20.

# 2010 THE YEAR OF CHANGE

The year 2010 brought about a lot of changes in the lives of my family and me. On February 11, 2010, my mother died. She had lived with us for nearly twenty-five years and went home to be with the Lord transitioning from her bed in our home to her home in glory. My mother, whom we affectionately called Sweetie, had been experiencing health challenges for years. But her memory was never impaired. She was a reliable source for accurately recalling past events about friends, church, or family. She had a severe case of arthritis in both knees, but she continually pressed her way out to church on Sunday mornings. She always had her rides lined up consisting of men from her church. Mr. Frank McDonald, Mr. Charles Stukes, Mr. Wilbur Edison, and even her beloved pastor, whom she loved deeply, Rev. Horace Cross, were always willing to pick her up and bring her back home. All these men understood that I had my obligations at the various churches where I served as the minister of music. Sweetie was in the hospital at the end of January 2010 when she was diagnosed with the possibility of having pancreatic cancer. The doctors performed a biopsy but said it was too dangerous to perform surgery on her to take out what they said "maybe" cancer. The decision was made to let her live out her life, hoping that the tumor was benign and not malignant.

# THE THINGS I REMEMBER

After her hospital stay, because Sweetie couldn't move around and take care of herself, the recommendation was that she be transferred to the nursing home for rehabilitation. Instead, I received a call on my job telling me my mom was being discharged from the hospital to go home.

I remember being so shocked to get this phone call because the last I heard she was going to the nursing home for rehabilitation. Nevertheless, I brought her home to our house and settled her in the bedroom we had prepared for her. Due to her inability to move around, Teresa and I made every accommodation to make her comfortable. The truth is, without hesitation or reservation, we waited on her hand and foot. Teresa cooked, served, bathed, and did all she could do as if my mom was her own mom. Teresa even hurt her back due to bathing my mom, but she never stopped attending to her needs.

While sharing the responsibilities of caring for my mom, Teresa held down a full-time job working at Trinity Baptist Faith Diamond's school and daycare. My wife put in ten to twelve hours a day and still had the heart and mind to help take care of my mom. I took time off my job for weeks because my mom needed help around the clock. Sometimes my mom would call from her phone in the middle of the night because she needed something. Teresa had to be at work before 6:00 a.m., and after being up with my mom, I would wake up to take Teresa to work. Then I would come back home to do all I could do for my mom.

On February 10, 2010, as we were about to go to bed, I went in to see if my mom needed anything. I must confess that we were tired but determined to do all we could do for Sweetie. Sweetie called me on our phone line and asked for some water so she could take a fluid pill. She said to me, "If I don't take the fluid pill, fluid will build up around my heart, and it could kill me." I watched her take the pill and said: "Love you, girl." I reminded her to drink the Ensure vitamin drink because she wasn't eating the way she should.

I slept so well for the first time in a while because my phone never rang. Teresa and I got up about 5:00 a.m., and she prepared to go to work. I had to take her to work, so I told Teresa, "I'm going to check on Sweetie before we go." I went to my mom's room, and the first thing I noticed was the television was still on, and it was loud. I looked at Sweetie lying there peacefully with her fingers on her chin as if she was thinking about something. Then, I remember thinking that something just didn't seem right.

I looked at her, and it appeared that she was not breathing. I turned the television down and called her name. There was no answer. I touched her hand that she had resting on her chin to wake her up, and the hand just fell to the bed. I kept calling her and felt her arms, and they felt really cool. I went into our bedroom and said to my wife, who was in the bathroom, "Sweetie is gone." My wife said, "Gone where Edward?" "I think Sweetie is dead," I said with my voice breaking. We went together to her room and discovered that our mother had fallen asleep in our house and woke up in God's house in the early hours of February 11, 2010. I called "911."

I was instructed to try to give her mouth-to-mouth resuscitation. When I tried to open her mouth, it was stiff and sealed shut. It really hurt to feel my mom's mouth sealed and her body cool. She was gone. This woman who gave birth to me at the late age of forty-four, this woman who was a mother and a father to me, this woman who taught me how to tie a necktie, my mother was gone. Sweetie Alberta Wilson, at the blessed age of ninety-eight, had moved in with God. I must confess that I lost it. What I knew would probably happen one day in our home had happened, and it hurt. I cried, my wife cried, my children, woke up with plans to go to school, but instead, they cried over this beautiful ninety-eight-year-old woman called that they called "Granma."

I remember our daughters getting up to find out that their grandmother was in bed asleep in Jesus. They cried with tears of sadness. I remember the paramedics coming to the house accompanied by

## THE THINGS I REMEMBER

the Chesapeake police. They came in and were really concerned and considerate of the situation. I was asked to get her identification card. As I went into her room and saw her lying there so peacefully, I remembered the last words she heard me say to her, "I Love you, girl." There she laid, no more pain, no more sickness, no more arthritis, no more wheelchairs. The policeman asked for the phone number of my job, and he contacted my boss, Mr. Ed Godwin, to inform him of what was going on. At some point, we contacted our cousins Jackie, Rona, and Sarah. We also called our dear friends Avis and James Hinton.

I remember making the call to Pretlow and Sons Funeral Home to come and pick up the remains. The owner, Mr. Richard Pretlow, who had seen me playing the music at many funerals, was surprised when he came into the house and saw me. He came and took my mom away. I remember standing outside as he rolled her body down the walkway to the driveway. So many memories flooded my soul. I remember saying to myself, "My wife and I did all we could do."

It wasn't long before the telephone started ringing. So many calls came in offering condolences to us. On the day that Sweetie transitioned, a homegoing was held for Mrs. Lucille Hails. My mom's pastor, Rev. Horace Cross, who was like a son to her, later described what it was like for him upon hearing about my mom's passing. He stated that he was scheduled to participate in Mrs. Hail's funeral. But he was so overcome with grief, he felt he could not participate in the service. He shared that he didn't want to reach out to me because he knew I would hear the overwhelming sorrow in his voice. He was afraid he would upset me, but Maria, his wife, told him to "get himself together." He said that Maria told him, "Peterman needs you, and you've got to get it together." On the same day of my mom's passing, around 1:00 in the afternoon, the family of Mrs. Lucille Hails visited my home, as well as Mrs. Evelyn Bazemore and her daughters. With Mrs. Evelyn was her

## 2010 THE YEAR OF CHANGE

grandson and my friend and brother, Rod Banks. All throughout the week, people came and brought food and love and shared precious memories.

As we made preparations for Sweetie's funeral, we were informed by her Pastor, Rev. Cross, that Sweetie had already made her funeral arrangements. We learned that she had made several drafts because individuals she wanted to participate in her funeral had already died. When we were told this, we just laughed because we could see her making the changes,

As we looked through her insurance papers, we found her plans and planned her funeral accordingly. That was the sadness of 2010. My mom was so well-loved by her grandchildren to the point that on the nights of what tradition calls "the sitting up" (people came to visit and support the family), Sweetie's bedroom and bed in which she died was the hangout place for my children and their young friends. No fear, just love. A few months later, if Sweetie had lived, she would have seen the birth of her fourth great-grandchild, Raynald David III, the joy of 2010. Raynald David III, or as we call him "Trey," was born in Chesapeake Regional Hospital to my daughter and son-in-law Ray. This took us from sadness to joy in our family as we celebrated a newborn. This boy is the spitting image of me when I was Sweetie's little boy.

Then, in August 2010 came a very emotional hurt in the lives of our family. We resigned our membership and duties from the church where we had worked, served, and committed ourselves for many, many years. My wife worked there first as the academy administrator, and then she took a position as a teacher. As I said earlier, my wife worked ten to twelve hours and more each day. When she was the head administrator, she was responsible for many families becoming members of this church by inviting them to the worship service. She worked long hours with pride. My wife opened the academy in the morning and was there when it closed in the late evening. There were many days she drove the school van that provided transportation for the academy students and students who attended the public school.

I served as the minister of music and activity coordinator. I birthed several ministries. I organized the Greeters Ministry, which consisted of males and females responsible for greeting churchgoers with a smile whenever they were on duty. Also, I birth The Builders Ministry, a group of members who were carpenters and plumbers and other professions. This ministry was responsible for totally renovating a house owned by the church, transforming it into a bookstore, additional classrooms for the academy, and an office for me. I also birthed the Equipment Travel Team. These were the fellows that helped load and unload equipment when the pastor and the church had outgoing engagements. This team proved to be invaluable. For nearly one year, church services were conducted weekly late Sunday afternoons in a middle school in southern Chesapeake. This required loading up the sound equipment and the music equipment and setting things up for the service. After the service, we had to put everything back on the bus, take them back to the church, and set things back up for our next Sunday service. They also transported equipment to various churches during our outgoing engagements. These fellows were a blessing helping in this area. I also recruited some fantastic fellows to serve on the Audio/Video Ministry or, as we called it, the A.V. Ministry. God blessed me to form a team of folks who would make video commercials advertising the church's upcoming activities. I brought in one of the area's well-known radio personalities, Brother Donald L. Eason, to read the scripts to be played on Sunday mornings.

Even on my job, my boss was aware that if the pastors of my church needed me, I would quickly leave work to accommodate their needs. Teresa and I never missed an engagement or service, whether it was in-house or outgoing. It was an honor to work on the tires for the families of our leaders because of the love I had and still have for them. Funeral services were always held (and still

## 2010 THE YEAR OF CHANGE

are held) at eleven o'clock because that was the time of my lunch break, and I could get away from my job without losing too much leave. I remained as the minister of music throughout September 2010 to allow time to find another minister of music.

My wife and I were always there. Anywhere we were needed, we tried to fulfill that need with loyalty and respect. We gave our "ALL" to this ministry and the leaders. We gave our time, talent, gifts, finance, and most of all, our "TRUE" commitment, loyalty, and love to the ministry and to the leaders. I'm not bragging about what we did because we committed ourselves to God and the ministry wholeheartedly. As previously stated, Teresa and I are no longer a part of this ministry but be assured that we continue to love them and that they continue to love us.

Our personal income suffered greatly after leaving the ministry. But God blessed us with financial blessings on top of financial blessings. People would tell us that God spoke to them and told them to give to us. The stories that accompanied the giving warmed our hearts. So many gave out of love, including the members of my singing group, The Edward Wilson Ensemble. Then there was a gentleman who was a member of our former church who said he was working in his garden, and the Lord spoke to him, and he came over immediately in his gardening clothes and blessed us. Another former church member said she was in her classroom teaching, and the spirit spoke to her concerning our family. She told us to meet her at Walmart, and she gave us the money to buy groceries, more groceries, and more groceries. When we left this ministry, you must understand that it was a considerable decrease in our income, but God always came through for us, reminding us that "He had us" and was taking care of us." We were in a restaurant eating one day, and a gentleman came up to us and said, "Your meal is paid for." The Bible says, "Give, and it shall be given back to you." We gave our finances through tithes and offerings. We gave all suggested giving, including leadership birthdays, holidays, and love offerings.

We gave one hundred percent to the work of the ministry, participating in whatever and where our services were needed. We were obedient, and God is faithful.

Today the relationship has been restored and the love between the leaders and us remains. We are "always" happy to see each other. We've been back to the church several times to fellowship. I was honored to return to play the music for the mass choir and direct them in their "Old School Back in the Day Service." Man, we had so much fun! God has blessed us in more ways than we could even imagine.

Well, you may ask, "What happened." Just let me say time changed, things changed, people changed, we changed. Our season was over, and what seemed to be sour lemons in the lives of my family and me later became sweet lemonade because of the wonderful grace of God.

After leaving the ministry mentioned above, I went back to my home church in Bells Mill, Mount Lebanon Baptist Church. The Word was proclaimed, and it was medicine for the pain my wife, children, and I was experiencing. The church pastor didn't know that we were there, and the preached messages were as if he knew that we were there and knew what we were feeling in emotional pain.

We eventually became members of Mount Lebanon Baptist, now known as The Mount. It was where I was raised and saved as a young boy. We were welcomed with open arms as my wife, and I met with the leaders. The pastor said to me, "Rev. Peterman, do as God leads you to do even if he tells you to go back, but know that you and your family are welcome here." So, we stayed there and were fed with spiritual healing food for what we had gone through.

God healed our pain, and we were led to deposit our membership and support at the Church of the Living God. And that is where we are today until God says differently. On January 3, 2014, by the power vested in my pastor, Dr. Sarah Eason Williams (and my cousin), I was ordained, set aside to do the kingdom's work as Pastor of Music and Media. Having her gifts of preaching and teaching recognized by our pastor, my wife was licensed to preach the gospel on July 6, 2014, and currently serves as the dynamic, spirit-filled, anointed praise & worship leader.

The pastor of our church is my cousin, mentioned earlier in this book, Dr. Sarah E. Williams. We are supporting the ministry there with all our hearts. Since being there, God has used us to organize a praise team that serves two Sundays each month. I organized a men's choir, praise team, and a youth choir which sings one Sunday a month. We were instrumental in acquiring the church building, parsonage, and a double-wide trailer used as a fellowship hall which sits on 2.5 acres of land. A good friend of mine, Rev. Vernon Jones, informed me that the church may possibly be for sale. We donated a stainless-steel stove and refrigerator. The church logo, which I designed, is proudly displayed on the podium, and imprinted on church T-Shirts. I have drawn plans for a new wing consisting of offices, restrooms, a fellowship hall, and a gymnasium. I was proudly instrumental, with the assistance of Brother Joey Harris, in the church purchasing an A100 Hammond organ with a Leslie tone cabinet. We've devoted ourselves to supporting our cousin, Dr. Sarah Eason Williams, in any way we can. It's all because we love God, and we're so grateful for Him being who he is and for Him allowing us to be who we are in Christ.

Teresa and I are both retired and enjoying God's grace and mercy. In my retirement from Chesapeake Public Schools, I find myself filled with joy being with my beautiful wife day in and day out. We never get tired, never get bored, never want to have "me" time because we enjoy the "us" time so much. As part of our day, we have praise and worship together each morning, including prayer and three different confessions. In this, we've found tremendous growth in our walk with God as a couple and individually. I admonish all couples to pray together and stay together and put their trust and hope in God. Encourage your children to implement these attributes into their lives and relationships.

If I were to choose a song that best tells my story, it would be Andre Crouch's "Through It All," which has the following lyrics:

*I've had many tears and sorrows I've had questions about tomorrow*
*There've been times I didn't know right from wrong*
*But in every situation God gave me sweet consolation*
*That my trials only come to make me strong*

*I thank God for my mountains, and I thank Him for my valleys*
*And we thank Him for all the things he's brought me through*
*For if I'd never had a problem,*
*I'd never know that God could solved them*
*I'd never know what faith in God could do*

*"BUT" through it all, through it all,*
*I've learned to trust in Jesus, I've learned to trust in God*
*Through it all, through it all, I've learned to depend upon his Word.*

**So, this is my story, and this is my song**
**Praising my savior all the day long**
**Praise God for life living in the village called Bells Mill**

THE END

# EPILOGUE

I find myself now at the end of the year 2021 living the life of retirement that so many people work so hard to accomplish. As I stated earlier, my wife and I are both retired after years of being protected and guarded by God's angels of mercy on our various jobs. "Through many dangers toils and snares I have already come, twas grace that kept me safe thus far and grace will lead me home." My wife and I have grown and are still growing closer to God and to each other after forty-three years of marriage. We share each day in our daily devotions which we have done for many years. When illnesses come up, we find ourselves laying hands on each other as we agree in prayer for the manifestation of total healing that was purchased over two thousand years ago on mount Calvary. We do our best to support our church, The Church of the Living God in any way we can with our gifts, talents, and our finances. Our Pastor Dr. Sarah E. Williams felt in her spirit the call to elevate my wife and me in ministry to serve as Executive Pastors of the church.

    Teresa is our praise and worship leader and I serve as the Pastor of music and media of our church. Teresa blessed me with a new electric Clavinova grand piano. I get such joy in playing and writing God inspired music. God has truly kept us through life's trials. We have learned no matter what the obstacle, we can do all things through Christ who continues to strengthen us. I can honestly say that I do love my wife like Christ loves the church and gave His life for it. I've told Teresa many times that I would quickly lay down my life for her. She is a wonderful, beautiful, loving, Godly, spirit filled woman of God and I am so blessed to have her as my wife. And I know that she loves me, and she supports me in "everything" I do to the glory of God. She is my encourager, my inspiration, my prayer partner, and my best friend. We've raised our four daughters to be beautiful and sweet young ladies. We have instilled in them to recognize and know the power of God and we encourage them to use the power God has given them through His word. The word of God tells us, "Greater is He that is in us than he that is in the world."

Each of our daughters is now grown and on their own. Our oldest daughter Keisha whom I refer to as a hard-working woman of wisdom is married to a loving family man named Lamans Fuller or as we call him "Monzie." They have blessed us with three grandchildren, Aayla, Alaynah, and Ryan. They reside in Chesapeake, Virginia. Our next oldest daughter is Sherita who as I mentioned is the youth minister of our church. Sherita is a chemistry teacher in the Portsmouth Public School system. She is married to a wonderful, loving husband and family man named Raynald David II. They have blessed us with two beautiful grandchildren, Raynald David III (Trey) and Rayah. They also reside in Chesapeake, Virginia. I'm blessed to have the best sons-in-law in the world because they are both loving, family men who love and support their families and most of all, because both of them love the Lord Jesus Christ and have received Him as their personal savior. Our next daughter is Ashley. Ashley is not married but she is an artist and a fashion designer. There have been many who have come to her and asked her to design and make prom dresses and other special occasion gowns. She has made wedding gowns which she designed for brides, and we are so proud of her gift of fashion designing. Ashley works for the government, and she resides in Chesapeake near the home we lived in for twenty-four years not too far from our daughter Keisha. Our youngest daughter is Teresa

EPILOGUE

(Nikki) Wilson. Nikki is the baby of our girls and she works for a mortgage company. Nikki's passion is singing. She can sing all day and all night. Although the youngest of the four she is the tallest of the girls. Keisha and Ashley are in a tight race being the shortest. Nikki lives in the city of Norfolk, Virginia.

All of our daughters are gifted singers and I love it when they come together and sing with such beautiful harmony. Each and every Father's Day I simply ask for my wife to cook me her fried chicken smothered in her gravy and my daughters to sing a few songs for me. As I look at the many family pictures on each of the walls in our home, I can see how God has blessed me and my family. For each of our daughter's birthdays, my wife will cook whatever meal they desire to have. We all come together and celebrate with a delicious meal as we sing and have fun. At Christmas time we celebrate by exchanging gifts after we pull our names out of the bag, thus determining whose secret Santa we will be. We try to make sure when we are all together to share our thoughts and thanksgiving to God and take Holy Communion in our home. I must confess that I've been truly blessed with a beautiful, loving, and caring family. When there is a need for any member of the family circle, we all come together and try to fulfill that need. God "IS" good.

As far as the village Bells Mill is concerned, I find myself driving through Bells Mill quite often. As I travel through Bells Mill, I find myself in my heart and mind traveling down the streams of time. Precious memories, how they linger, how they ever flood my soul. With my eyes on a lot of properties, I see new homes built, but in my heart, I see the original homes I saw as a child. On the property on the corner of Bells Mill Road and Alexander Lane, I see with my eyes many beautiful homes but in my heart, I see the old Bells Mill Elementary School. As I drive down Luther Street, the street that I lived on from my birth until my junior high school days, I see with my eyes asphalt pavement but in my heart, I see a street made of rocks and tar. I also see with my eyes several new homes built on Luther Street, but in my heart, I see the homes I dwelt in playing with my childhood playmates. On Aberdeen Lane where my Aunt Laura and Uncle Arthur Eason lived, I see with my eyes smooth black asphalt pavement, but in my heart, I can see the graveled lane that only one car could drive on at a time. When I see with my eyes strangers leaving out of or going into the houses I use to dwell in as a child I can see in my heart the villagers who use to live there but they have either moved to a new home here on earth or their new home in heaven. Changes have taken place in Bells Mill as well as other black villages or communities in Chesapeake, Virginia but one thing that has not, and I pray will not change, is still called Bells Mill.

From Bells Mill to Elizabeth Court Town Houses, to Harbour North Apartments, to Fernwood Farms, to Mill Creek, to Holly Point Apartments, God has been and still is our provider and our keeper and our protector. As I have had the opportunity to reflect back on my life living in the village called Bells Mill to my age today of sixty-six, I can truly say in the famous words of a dear friend who recently passed away named James (Butch) Garris that "God has been so good to me". There is a song that was sung by the late Mahalia Jackson that said:

*God is so good to me - God is so good to me*
*I don't serve Him as I should - I don't deserve all of His good*
*So many things are not as they should be - "But"*
*God is so good to me.*

I will forever praise Him with the gifts He has given me. My wife will forever praise Him with the gifts He has given her. We've also encouraged our children and our grandchildren to give back to God what gifts He has given to them. The song says, "All things come of Thee oh Lord and of Thine own have given Thee."

# EPILOGUE

I pray that this book has in some way encouraged somebody in some way. I hope you found laughter in the true stories I've shared. I hope this book placed a smile on your face despite your life's circumstances. I hope it has been instrumental in letting somebody know that life is nothing without God. For those who may have read this book and who lived in Bells Mill, I pray that it brought back pleasant memories of the way we were and the way it was. Thank you for taking the time out to read about "The Things I Remember." May I leave you with the words written by Rev. Andre Crouch:

*I've had many tears and sorrows*
*I've had questions for tomorrow*
*There've been times I didn't know right from wrong*
*But in every situation*
*God gave blessed consolation*
*That my trials come to only make me strong*

*I thank God for the mountains*
*I thank Him for the valleys*
*I thank Him for the storms he brought me through*
*For if I'd never had a problem*
*I wouldn't know that God could solve them*
*I'd never know what faith in God can do*

*Through it all, through it all*
*I've learned to trust in Jesus, I've learned to trust in God*
*Through it all, through it all*
*I've learned to depend upon His word.*

May God bless you and keep you is my prayer.

Rev. Edward J. (Peterman) Wilson

# THE VILLAGE ROLL CALL "AS I KNEW THEM"

These are the names of people that I knew and remember in the village of bells mill. I started from one of Bells Mill and took my mental flight down Bells Mill Road and its off streets. If I missed any, please charge it to my memory and not to my heart. I learned so many Dos and Don'ts from these folks.

Mr. Mrs. Chuck & Lucille Roberts
Mr. Mrs. Lorenzo & Anniebell Holley
Mr. Mrs. Colon & Hilda Simmons
Mrs. Annie Edmonds
Mr. Mrs. Cle & Mary (Bug) Bell
Mrs. Rosa McDonald
Mrs. Elsie Ricks
Mr. Mrs. Buster & Lottie Bell
Mr. Mrs. Bill & Doll Chesson
Mr. Mrs. Ed & Pauline Bell
Miss. Elsie Small
Mrs. Emmaline Bell
Mr. Mrs. Earl & Myrna Bell
Rev. & Mrs. James & Sadie Alexander
Mr. Mrs. Peaco & Mary Williams
Mr. Mrs. Jo-Jake & Ida Riddick

THE THINGS I REMEMBER

Mrs. Eva Edmonds
Mr. Mrs. Charlie & Goldie Walker
Mr. Mrs. Herley & Rosa Satterfield
Rev. Mrs. Arthur & Lyll Harper
Mrs. Bessie Ricks
Mr. Mrs. Ira & Janie Cuffee
Mr. Mrs. Curtis & Mary Turner
Mr. Mrs. Hosea & Mary Davis
Mr. Mrs. Albert Wilson
Mr. Mrs. George & Wanza Moyler
Mr. Mrs. Raymond & Rose McDonald
Mrs. Hattie Todd
Miss. Cap Bell
Miss. Theresa Bell Felton
Mr. Mrs. William & Rosa Bell
Mr. Mrs. Alton & Alfreda Batts
Mr. Frank Chesson
Mr. Mrs. Al & Pearl Tendall
Mr. Mrs. Alton & Rosa Felton
Mrs. Elsie Mae
Mr. Mrs. William & Vann Alexander
Mrs. Lillian Williams
Mr. Mrs. Paul & Ruth
Mr. Mrs. George & Georgia Roberts
Mr. Mrs. Arthur & Laura Eason
Mr. Mrs. Morris & Carol Ethridge
Mr. Mrs. Roosevelt Townsend
Mr. Mrs. Willie & Mable Townsend
Mr. Mrs. Henry & Mary Hargrove
Miss. Harriet Bryant
Mr. Mrs. Jupiter Roberts
Mr. Mrs. Pewee & Vernice Mitchell
Mr. Mrs. Dewey & Nancy Fennel

# THE VILLAGE ROLL CALL "AS I KNEW THEM"

Mr. Mrs. Rubean & Hattie Griffin
Miss. Luvenia & Miss Gloria Peterson
Mr. Sam Peterson
Mr. Mrs. Harmon & Ruth Johnson
Mr. Mrs. James & Mary Johnson
Mr. Mrs. Henry & Alveria Pretlow
Mrs. Mr. Sonny & Doris Sykes
Mrs. Flora Locker
Mr. Mrs. Roosevelt & Chesson
Mr. Mrs. Charles & Larue Davis
Mr. Big Jo & Marie Davis
Mr. Foster (Store Owner)
Mr. Mrs. Walter & Lillie Mae Jones
Miss. Fannie Flemmons
Mrs. Alberta McDonald
Mr. Mrs. Wilbur Edison
Mr. Mrs. Seth & Odessa McDonald
Mrs. Mammie Valentine
Mrs. Emmett & Sophia Alexander
Mr. Mrs. Tilt & Fidella Alexander
Mr. Mrs. Henry & Lizzie Corprew
Mr. Mrs. Bob & Ruth Massey
Mr. Mrs. Ed & Mary McDonald
Mr. Mrs. Eldret & Leola Watson
Mr. William & Margret Richardson
Mr. Mrs. Edward Sanford
Mr. Mrs. Sambo & Mamie Moyler
Mr. Mrs. Bishop Beatrice Bell
Mrs. Mary Moore
Mr. Mrs. Horace & Elsie Mae Alexander
Mr. Mrs. Linwood & Aivonia Manning
Mr. Mrs. Ed & Kathrine Burton
Mrs. Vernice Leggett

# THE THINGS I REMEMBER

Mr. Mrs. Vernon & Alice Bell
Miss. Madie Alexander
Mr. Mrs. Morris & Essie Mae Ethridge
Mrs. Thelma Wilkes
Mr. Mrs. Henry & Rosa Manley
Mrs. Mildred Satterfield
Mr. Mrs. Rodney & Shirley Creekmore
Mr. Mrs. James & Mary Evans
Mr. Mrs. Howard & Lizzie Satterfield
Mrs. Lizzie Mae Bell
Mr. Mrs. Frank & Alice Stukes
Mr. Mrs. Bro & Maude Moore
Rev. Mrs. John & Edna Clark
Mrs. Ida (Plum Pie) Ferebee
Mrs. Sarah McGlone
Mr. Mrs. Sam & Helen Coker
Mr. Mrs. Elmer & Emma Bell
Mr. Mrs. Snoop & Adell Harper
Mr. Mrs. Hosea & Cherry Durham
Mr. Mrs. Mike & Pearl Holley
Mr. Lloyd Lamb & His Siter Thelma
Mr. Mrs. Harrison & Lena Kealling
Mrs. Matron Ivey Beckett
Mrs. Bessie Smith

CPSIA information can be obtained
at www.ICGtesting.com
Printed in the USA
BVHW030327150622
639757BV00004B/15